#IKAW

A bunch of run-on sentences about being kinda normal with the crazy-awesomeness of my life.

ALLYSON BICKEL

DEDICATION

To all who have been in my past, present or future, who have created a page or chapter in my life, and allow me to express myself. Whether you like it or not, you have shaped who I am right this second.

To my Kickin Asphalt fan squad who pushed for more and were very persistent. Katie, Nicole, Randi - your positive reinforcement grew me wings. To my ride-or-die friends - Hailey, Jess, Oatmeal and Krista that constantly remind me how awesome I am and that I am not one bit crazy. To my parents who always have my back, good or bad, and who taught me to follow through and finish when you start something.

All Book Photo Credits: Kim Hanson
All Hair Design: Melissa Boyce

CONTENTS

INTRODUCTION

Surgeon General's Warning: The contents of this book may be crude, way too honest and offensive. If you find things too offensive, then you need to find a sense of humor or a different book to read. If you feel at any point in time I am writing about our relationship, I probably am, and you are probably an idiot.

I am so much rolled into one. I can truly say that I love myself. It has taken a while to get here, but I do. Despite my complaining in this book about my struggles, I'm pretty good most days. You work so hard on one person for so long, that finally, you accept who you are and everything just makes sense. Sure, there are bad days where you feel like a failure, but ultimately, you look in the mirror everyday and like what you see. God sure is awesome, how he instills confidence in everyone and we are all so different. We are all different sizes, shapes and genders. Some of us are really ugly and some of us are really beautiful. We are all unique, we all have a gift, and we all deserve a chance.

Everyone is an inspirational speaker these days. Anyone can post quotes and positive reinforcements on Facebook with a great picture. I am not claiming to be that person. I am not. I do not claim to be of any knowledge or know many facts. I simply speak my truth. I am so honest it makes me sick sometimes. This book is based on my experiences in life. When I tell you I have the best idea, or explain my ideas, I do not claim to know best. My main purpose is to let you know that you aren't alone. My struggles are actually your struggles and yours are mine. Life is hard people, let's laugh, let's cry and let's celebrate the hot mess express that we are. All we can do is do the best we can, everyday. If your best is Netflixing 'College Friends" all day, then play on playa. You have the choice to do what you want, when you want. You're a fucking adult, so live your life like you are one. My blogs have been my release, and now this book is part of my life story. This is a collection of failures, tests, celebrations and 100% pure life lived.

If you are an English guru, try to look the other way when you look at how I use commas and italics. Sometimes I just add things because it looks 'pretty' or I believe it helps tell my story how I am speaking ;)

#IAM

Mother. Lover. Blogger. Realist with a side of daydream. Loud Music In A Car. Smiling. Cuddler. Rain storms. Big heart. Weights. Yes Girl. Part Mexican. Tattoos. Traveling. Coffee. Saving money. Black and white images. Coffee mugs. Art. Live Music Makes Me Cry. Miller Park. Sports. Working out. YMCA. Coffee.

#BEFOREYOUSTART

There is no wrong or right way to read this book. Read it one chapter at a time, or one hashtag at a time. Life doesn't always make sense, therefore, neither will I.

If you take anything from this book.... please take:

1. The scale is a magical tool, it does not tell you your worth.
2. Carbs ARE your friend, I don't care what Brenda says.
3. You are worthy of love.

4. Don't waste your time on idiots or anyone who makes you feel mentally crazy.

5. Choose your tribe wisely.

6. Laugh at yourself.

If you like this book you need to watch:

1. *The Mindy Project*

2. *New Girl*

3. *College Friends*

4. *Drinking Buddies*

5. *Young and Hungry*

#BODY IMAGE

#INTROTOMYBRAIN101

My physical appearance has always been under construction. Since declaring in 7th grade, my New Years Resolution was to weigh 98 lbs, for God knows why, I've been chasing that neon rainbow. Not quite as drastic, but for some reason for over 5 years, my dream number has been 185. Is that too hard to ask? Yes, it is. I mean, a number is a number, and most people who weigh what they weigh, don't look like they weigh that? Unless when in reality, you look at me and see Lizzo and when I look in the mirror I see Beyonce? Then yes, yes my number is accurate. No offense to either ladies, ya'll got it going on.

For as long as I can remember, I've been in the gym. I remember hitting up the "nautilus", as they called it when I was 11 or 12, with my dad and it hasn't stopped since then. I've tried almost every diet in America: celery soup, keto, Weight Watchers, starvation, binging, intermittent fasting and counting calories. My current plan and life goal is to be satisfied, happy and content. I want to have complete control over food, because I'm a binger. I binge when I'm sad or stressed or don't have a plan to save my soul. I also eat crappy when it's anywhere from

5-8 days before payday because my grocery budget has been long gone by then. Also sometimes, if I don't have a solid head on my shoulders; one taste of a brownie with chocolate frosting on it will send me through the roof and I'll keep eating until I find the bottom of the WHOLE pan. And even then, I'll want more. So my success is sloth speed, but I'll take it, if it means having control.

#SPEEDS

I have 3 fitness/weight loss speeds. Walking disaster. Half assing. Balls to the walls.

#WALKINGDISTASTER

If I don't have a legit plan in place for eating and working out, look out, I'm a disaster. There is no limit to what I will eat and no plan when I grocery shop, except whatever the F I feel like. No thought. Sometimes I eat three grilled cheeses, sometimes I eat a box of cosmic brownies and sometimes I just eat all day long, with maybe 1 hour between eats. I'm not even hungry. This my friend, is the worst feeling ever. Usually this day happens when I'm SUPER stressed out, or I'm super over tired or hungover. And sometimes this happens because I had a bad day before, and my body is like in crazy crack mode yearning for another cosmic or salty french fry. Sometimes it happens, because when I am on my other speed - balls to the walls and I slip up once, per say, eating ONE M&M. I go ape shit. My brain alarm goes off like in "Inside Out" and I basically set myself on fire. Major destruction. Which truly recently happened for a solid 6 months of no give a damns and I stopped lifting kinda because what was the point? I mean it wasn't all day long eating, but it was crap and also summer, so I drank a lot of margaritas and didn't workout as much because I didn't eat well.

#HALFASSING

Every single day, I'll wake up, eat healthy, lunch comes, eat decent, snack on fruit, supper, then about 8 pm, it's eat everything, followed by a snack bowl in bed with wine and a "Good night, we'll try again tomorrow."

Those are the days I'm wishing I was dedicated. I know exactly what I'm doing, but I just don't care quite enough yet. Or tell myself it's ok. So everyday I either overeat at night or something happens during the day, I'm starting over. For instance, start on a Monday, do good, but then something comes up every single day to derail you, and I let it derail me. I feel like I'm in *Groundhog's Day* and start over everyday. Like, I consciously want to be back on track, I just haven't really looked in the mirror hard enough, or made an eating plan or grocery shopped quite good enough yet. And excuses. If I was a fitness person or nutrition guru, I would plain out tell my clients, life happens. It's ok to eat two brownies, it's ok to eat out for breakfast and lunch and dinner and not feel guilty. I need them to tell me that they, too, are human and aren't cookie cutter perfect. That would take off a lot of pressure in the beginning starting something new, over and over and over. I recently told my trainer that I had a horrible sugar filled, dessert infested day. But honestly I woke up not feeling guilty, because I let myself have that day. And she was proud of me. And I was also. Woke up and kept going.

#BALLSTOTHEWALLS

This happens, shit I don't know when the last time this happened. But what it looks like is: eat lettuce, chicken, fish, eggs, popcorn, water, oatmeal, lean cuisines, baked potatoes. This will last for about two days, then insert:: set myself on fire:: and it's over. Too restrictive. I get so pissed off prior, that I'm like "That's it Allyson, let's eat things that won't last long just to get pushed back into walking disaster." Just like rotating around the sun, it's inevitable.

#FEARS

I'm so afraid that when you are first starting to dial in to eating better and working out again, you are starting at point A essentially, and it's so easy to go backwards and lose my small/short progress because I'm so fresh in the journey. One slip up could be one three day binge session where I would have to burn those calories off before getting any other progress. Losing two lbs is so fucking hard, that when I do lose it, it's a slap in the face, because essentially that is a two day binge for me and poof, back up there. I told my then trainer my fear of starting and failure and she compared it to an alcoholic who also had that same fear, but the fear of slipping a drink. And then all her walls come crashing down and she's back where she started. But think about it. You're NOT back where you started, unless the cycle continues. You are where you are. You can choose to realize you made a mistake, and turn it around, or you can keep going backwards, but one slip up doesn't take away all of the hard work and logging and working out I've been doing the past three months.

Me talking:: Truly, is eating three brownies instead of one a slip up? I mean, it could be, or you could just move on and call it life:: She said it much better than I just did. But for anyone who has this fear also, it's real. It's a real fear. The fact that my progress is sloth speed, scares the crap out of me because of the easy slips from bad habits. But during this sloth speed, I am also creating control habits, dedication habits, self love habits, stress habits, food shopping habits, eating habits, workout habits, and trying to bury the binge habits and self sabotage habits. Eat the fucking cookie and move on. Go to the pot luck dinner and have two plates of food and carry the fuck on. Enjoy your life. Eating off your radar is inevitable, it's what makes life, life. Don't be that girl, showing up to the party with her own whole wheat buns. Live a little. That was some real shit. #dontbethatgirl

#CORONAVIRUS19

All bets are off. ::sets self on fire::

#WEIGHTWATCHERS

Over the past few years, Weight Watchers has been the only thing that has worked for me. But it was like four to five months of balls to the walls and I was seriously hungry the whole time, I could hear my aching ribcage ask my stomach for a Happy Meal. I know it's just another calorie deficit plan, but it's a little more fun than counting cals. It's like how can I make this meal close to five points errryday.

Weight Watchers is great. They give you a daily 'point' allowance, and a weekly 'point' allowance. Which all reset weekly. Thing is, girlfrand, you don't know me. Those weekly points were gone on day two. Kinda like when you get your paycheck and then two days later you are like wtf. It was mad crazy. So from day three to seven was like drinking my own spit and eating fruits and veggies, basically digging myself a coffin, when I'd rather be eating a muffin. Ba-da- ching! I'm so funny. There was zero point food, where you could eat as much as you wanted, you know, by still using your brain. And turns out, I wasn't using my brain, because I wasn't eating three bananas in a row (zero points) like my ribcage was trying to tell me. I lost 17 lbs in 13 weeks? Was like hella fly, size 12 jeans. And I was able to keep that off for about two to three months. Then it was fight or flight, counting cals and working out. Then of course, after a few months of not doing Weight Watchers, you go back and try it again, fail, quit, then try again, then fail, quit. Again, just rotating around the sun. I can't even hate on Weight Watchers because some people know how to work the system and lose accurately. Cheers to them.

#ENOUGHISENOUGH

You ever wake up and think to yourself... ok fatty, enough is enough, you have to do the hard work. The work that only a few can do. The work that keeps you away from social gatherings for longer than three hours so you aren't judged when you whip out an apple or fry up an egg, because they are already logged in my fitness pal. You need to get your shit together, because no one is going to do it for you. You have to tell those pants who is the GodDamn Queen, you have to focus so hard, you have to hold yourself down when you want to finish the ice cream. It's not that I can't have it, it's that it's not going to help me. One bowl is enough.

#LITTLEGIRLATEMYTURKEYSUB

Keeping your diet on point is super freaking hard. I remember having tunnel vision with Weight Watchers over here for almost two solid weeks. High five, butt slap, chest bump. Weighed in - down two lbs. Great, wham bam - thank you ma'am. Guess what happened after my super awesome weigh in. Oh, life happened that's what. I left the kids at home real quick, call CPS I dare you. Weighed in at Weight Watchers and came right back. No children were harmed during this time. I had a whole day training on Youth Mental Health First Aid on a freaking Wednesday, which meant my points also started over on that day. Anyway, so I peeled and packed my own hard boiled eggs, a banana, an apple, and a protein bar. I asked my friend what was going to be for lunch, and she said subs. So immediately I was super stoked. I could count subs easily. Ok, ok so at the training there are baked chips... awesome, a cookie, which immediately that little punk ass cookie went back on the table. Not today baby Satan, not today. But guess what? The girl in front of me took the last turkey sub. This little girl, who is about as large as a six inch veggie sub took the last turkey, I could have cried. I should have said, "Oh look, a bird!" and grabbed it out of her hands. So I was dealt a club, a cold cut or ham. Like what was even in those. If you don't know, I'm allergic to

9

pork, so I can't eat ham. Or any kind of mixed sausage because they like to mix every little cute farm animal into sausage, especially pork toes. So I logged it in my app and it was 10 points, ok ok just breath. 10 points for a six inch sandwich that I didn't even want to eat. Funk that. But, you know, I'm so proper and kind that I devoured the whole thing. In two bites, like a dragon. And, I had the balls to log my mayonnaise and chips for seven extra points. I am only allowed 23 points a day, so I ate 17 at lunch, and three at breakfast that I couldn't regurgitate up. So supper was going to have to be zero points. But you know what? I was asked to wing night by my parents. So shit, ok, be normal and just go, get some free (love you mom and dad) food and be social. 32 points for six chicken wings. And I only got 6,000 steps from my morning to 7 pm at night because I was sitting in a chair all day. So if you haven't skipped this chapter already because you are like this girl is nuts, thank you. Long story short, I had weighed in today, meaning my points for the week started over that day and *I ate all my points* for the day, plus my fitness points, plus about 10 extra 'weekly' points. I wasn't happy. I had a point to this, just not sure I'm getting to where I wanted to go. Oh, yeah, life is hard and that right there, with the early on progress, is why fear sets into me and gives me anxiety. You can't control everything that happens around you. I've found that if I am hungry, I have to eat something, or I'll be a massive monster an hour or two later wondering what in the f@ck just happened. Juggling kids, work, friends, family, food, stress eating, trying to lose weight, trying to remember to wear pants every day. It's all hard. So what do we do? We prevail. We rise up. We actually go home and eat ice cream and call it a day. I know someone who is going to be walking 3.7 on the treadmill for 45 minutes tomorrow. Yeah boom, in yo face. ::Trips on her own feet as she does a hair flip and walks out the door:: update:: this said person did NOT do the treadmill as earlier mentioned, because, why?

#ITSANUMBERSGAME

I hate that with weight loss and goals, you *ALWAYS* want more. You lose five lbs, and end up eating yourself silly up 10. As humans, we are never satisfied, probably because there is always someone on tv subtly telling us we shouldn't be. Show of hands. When I was 194, I smelled 185. And you know what happened, I'm back to 210. With the help of a torn meniscus, and five months later plantars fasciitis, the big bad world made sure I snapped back into reality and indeed appreciated 194. Fuck. What I would give to feel 194 again (that was with my four to five months of successful, but hungry Weight Watchers). So right now, I'm trying not to focus on the scale and work on how I'm feeling. Like Yoda. My ultimate goal for years and years and years and years is 185. I have no idea why. That number just seems like a sexual dream. I don't give a crap I guess if you know my weight, because I'm at the point in my life where I know who I am, I know what I deserve, I know what I had, and I know what I'm capable of doing. I've had two kids, I've been married and divorced, I've been betrayed by men, I've seen defeat and somehow I can still get tail if I need to. So I'm basically a stone cold bad ass. Ok, somedays I feel like that, and some days I'm just happy the kids are still kept alive.

#NEVERSATISFIED

Sometimes I just need to bitch. I just need to release my demons, say what's been going on in my head to settle the score. Like for instance my grip on food. I mean my 'slip' on food. ::Insert geeky laugh:: I will never be happy. I just know it. Actually, I do know that I will be happy, once I lose 15 lbs. See, now do I care about weight or taking up less space on earth? Or am I satisfied just feeling 'really good'? I was so happy with my tight pants, my smaller waist, but guess what, I wanted more. I wanted MORE weight off, just seven more and I would have reached my ultimate goal of 185. Is that too fucking hard to ask for? Well, yes, yes it was. I don't even blame it on my aging bones and loss of metabolism. Cuz I'll tell ya what, "My metabolism is slowing down" is a fucking myth for those who are just too old to move. Boom. Truth bomb. Your metabolism doesn't slow down, you do, ya idiot.

It's my love/hate with food. It's my ever going emotions as a woman, as a mother, as a friend. I used to bartend, so if the locals conned me into having a beer after work with them (it's more like three or four, and I will blame age on this one), I'm four beers down and head through Taco Bell at 10 pm. Just once a month, but that once a month, derails my progress. Because usually Taco Bell isn't enough and I need a delicious dessert in bed, maybe with some combos or pretzels..... And I wake up the next morning, thinking wtf, why oh why, and sometimes continue the sabotage. Each week that I start my "diet", one day later something comes up and I'm eating chicken wings at Schooner (Bonnie, if you are reading this, I'd like to be your chicken wing poster pin up gal. Please. I already have the vision for a billboard). I know, you are thinking, well just get a salad. No shit Sherlock, but I always fight the struggle of 'be normal' and eat in moderation. I think that would be ok, if I ate good for like four or five days straight, and then ate the wings. But seriously.

What isn't always fun is when small children wake you up in the morning, before six am. Oh and add in daylight savings. So every daylight savings weekend I am totally the Walking Dead all weekend long. I do apologize to my kids, but what if, just what if, mommy asked to take a nap, and the kids could occupy themselves..... they let dad nap, in bribery of cash. But maybe all mommy has to bribe them with is Mac and Cheese. I guess I never tried, so it could work. Mom just needs a nap sometimes. I've taken about four naps in the total existence of my children breathing air. Guess what actually happened during one of those pleasant hours? My child woke me up and told me he thought a Sunflower was growing in his brain. I told him he was silly, but he came back about 10 minutes later very quiet and said it again. Alright, pal, what did you do? Turns out, he stuck a sunflower seed in his ear… no idea why, but we ended up in FastCare. You will be happy to know my child and the sunflower had flourished that summer.

Sometimes when I get really crabby at the kids, I say, "Ok, I love you so much, but you are making me mad." or "I love you so much, but just leave me alone."

I mean that's nice right? Puff up their self-esteem then gently tell them to get bent? I can't be the only one. So anyway, when I'm off my game, or stuck in the house because of winter, or don't go to stores (because help, they sell food there and stupid ass toys my kids want), I am stuck inside. I actually Yoko-Onoe'd (aka Marie Kondo) my basement one weekend and decluttered. But here's the real thing. Instead of decluttering I should have vacuumed, cleaned the toilets, dusted, there is so much dust I see daily, and I just walk by it, and wonder who is going to take care of that. Gaaaa. Hire a housemaid? I guess monthly, just to get dust and crevices mom NEVER gets. Sometimes I wonder if my ex would come over and detail my house if I wore a swanky apron... if that's wrong, I don't want to be right.

#THEBINGECODE

I've read a book called *The Binge Code*, by Alison C. Kerr. It was me to a T. We all want to succeed. I always want to succeed, but after wanting everything fitness related in the snap of a finger, I've finally realized it takes time. Bullshit amounts of time. I read a book about it and am doing the work, son. Eat 2300-2500 calories a day, gradually put in your treats daily so you never feel deprived to binge. Genius. So I've completed two whole weeks on this, binged three times, and lost five lbs, but this morning I woke up and had a four lb gain. WTF ever. I ate too legit to quit yesterday. Ok, lies, I stayed in my calorie goal, but I did carb load and had chocolate and caramels. Key words: calorie goal - So I seriously had to do everything in my will power to tell myself I'm doing the work, it's ok, I'm doing the work, it'll take time. Everything I could from jumping off the Menekaunee bridge. I bet if I took a shit...then weigh myself... but I didn't even obsess about that morning poo. I'm trying to create habits of self-positiveness rather than my usual just be fucking better you loser. Tracking my food and trying to keep it balanced. I know there are people out there. "You're too hard on yourself." "Just eat everything in moderation." Girlfriend, buzz off.

I trust everyone, I trust people I shouldn't trust because I trust so much. But this process of body image and acceptance and feeling good in your skin is the hardest pill to swallow. Allison is a recovering bulimic/binger and a psychologist. The whole point of her book is to get your eating under control. And after reading I was like, "Ok great, now how do I lose weight? " Never satisfied. To trust her process of eating 2300 calories a day and eating your favorite sweet daily makes sense and seems like child's play. But then my mind goes, but wait, I'm eating all these calories and shit I just binged for two days straight 5,900 calories. That shit is hella calorie expensive. But...... she writes about slowing the fuck down (my words, not hers) and realizing when you are about to go ape shit on your ice cream and snack cabinet, you need to take 10 minutes and meditate or clean something and the urge goes away. So far in one week I had 2 binge urges, one I did the 10 minute thing and cleaned and the other I took a bath and fell in love with baths. But last night I didn't really see it, until it happened. Omg. It started as buffalo pretzels and ranch, followed by sugar free candy (I'm wild) and protein balls, followed by wine and trail mix in bed. I have had way worse binges, but I'm tallying it up as a binge. So today I'm feeling sheepish. But am logging my intake and exercise and logging my binges I give into. Two in one whole week. So two I fought and two I took. She said they will never go away, but if I train my mind to create a new habit, they won't happen as much, and be less, as long as I'm giving my body what it needs in portions. Makes sense.

So the weight loss? If I eat 2300 calories a day and feed my beast, I should get to my body's happy weight. Seems simple. I'm one week in and down two lbs. It's probably water weight, but I'll be a hopeful romantic right now and take it as a win. Next week I'll be one more lb down and my food is under control and I'm not starving. That's how it works right? I choose to be optimistic... until I'm not. Lol.

#INJURIES

Whenever I picture injuries, I always think of someone dribbling up the court on a fast break, gets tripped or fouled, and tears his knee off. My injuries were just a reminder of 'your getting old.' One happened in the cusp of winter while doing a double under, torn meniscus. I heard it pop, I was scared, told everyone dramatically I needed surgery probably, turns out, it just needed time. Then early summer in a softball tournament, I couldn't walk by game four. Plantars Fasciitis. With the meniscus, I just scaled back lifting, didn't squat or deadlift as heavy and eventually, it did feel better within about four months. Now my feet on the other hand, it's been going on eight months and it's finally caught up to me mentally. I quit lifting for a month, but still played softball on Sundays which then made me gimpy on Monday-Thursday, feeling better, then doing it all over again on Sunday. But after softball, I slowly made progress. I don't know if I was getting used to the pain and it's going away slowly, or it's really going away. When things pile up, I end up having pity parties...sometimes for two months straight of eating crap and not giving a flying f*ck.

Now my problem is that I binge, and don't purge. I've tried almost every 'diet' known to man for at least the old 2 day trial (lol) where I then feel deprived and eat the whole house. Sometimes even making a quick trip to the store to get the most delicious food and eat it all. So my problem isn't that I can't lose weight, but wait, yes it is. It's that I am not keeping my body balanced with the way I diet that I go overboard and make unrealistic goals. Now fireworks did NOT just go off in my head knowing my goals were ridic, because hello, eating 1500 calories a day, is just a joke. I always hear, oh you'll be hungry, it's a part of the calorie deficit. Bullshit. I know in my heart of hearts, there is a way to lose weight and NOT feel like you are the wicked witch cringing in the tower as she gets a bucket of water thrown on her. But, I'm still figuring it all out.

#THESCALEISTHEDEVIL

I tried really hard for about two weeks to put the scale away. I tried to 'listen to my body.' And I'll tell you what. My body said girl, you better start eating salads. After about two weeks of not weighing myself, kinda eating well, but getting back to a consistent workout schedule, I jumped on the scale this morning. You know how you play the guessing game in your head of how bad it will be and then it's close to that number you pretend it's ok? Well I overshot three lbs. So I was pumped. But even the number I saw was like oh fuck, girlfran did some damage over the past four weeks. Yes, my pants are tight not because I had popcorn the night before or Mexican food two nights in a row, they are tight because I indeed gained a good eight lbs. So, what am I going to do about it? I am going to lose one lb. at a time.

So, I saw some photos from three years ago, and I was indeed obese-like. And then I saw a photo of myself last night, and thought damn girl, I hope you don't look like what you did three years ago. I contemplated texting my fitness buddy and fellow calorie obsessor with a nice photo comparison and see if she thinks I look the same, but I didn't. I will just do the work, but am definitely going to text her later and tell her fatty is on the wagon. That fucking wagon.

So let's get back to the scale. It can be a wonderful little friend or it can be the spawn of Satan. Usually, it's a mixture. I truly believe that when you obsess every day on losing weight, you lose your mind. But I also know that when you don't jump on the scale and just eat like a free range heffer, you also lose your mind. So I'd rather jump on the scale and see a plateau than an eight lb. weight gain. Am I right? So those of you who are shaking your head saying I'm too hard on myself. I'M NOT. I'm not over here crying and measuring spinach leaves. I'm simply letting you know that I am human, as are you and I need to get back on track. I am old enough to know that a number on the scale doesn't mean a lot, but simply a life tool. I will just call it a tool. Haha kinda like a few other things in my life that could be called a tool ;)

The scale is a good thing in the beginning, because you drop weight faster because you are losing water, salt, cupcakes, muffins, you know....... but when you start to plateau, THEN and ONLY THEN, go off of feeling. And if it gets so bad you must use the scale, use the scale. Let it make you happy that you actually ate a whole box of cake mix and only gained two lbs. Because we all know a good poop will take care of that.

So, to wrap it up, I don't claim to know everything, but I think I do. (jk) I dislike this quote also, but 'everyone is different' maybe Susie Sidesalad over there doesn't binge eat, and that's why I'm not friends with Susie Sidesalad.

#IMALLERGICTOPORK #KETOSUCKS
THINGS I HATE THAT I HEAR PEOPLE SAY. (Hate is a strong word)

I don't eat meat. I don't eat dairy. I don't eat gluten. I'm not eating sugar. I don't eat carbs. I'm on keto. Is that keto? Tofu is good. Oh, I'm not eating carbs right now. How much fat is in that? How many carbs are in that? It's non GMO. It's free range.

Do you know why I dislike those things? Because people are freaking cray. Including myself, obvi. I once did keto, lost seven lbs. And the whole time my breath smelled like an old man who kept eating onions and I actually self-induced a pork allergy because of all the bacon I consumed. No lie. It may be getting a little better. But straight up, can't eat brats, ham, bacon, some pepperoni, mixed ground beef/pork, or hotdogs. So yeah, pretty much the worst allergy ever. My lips puff up within a day and my top lip gets itchy and shed skin like a snake for a little over a week. You know how when people say they can't eat something that isn't really common, like pork, well that's the only weird one I can think of, people get all weirded out, and offended. Like I went on a date with a guy for breakfast, my meal came with bacon or sausage. But I guess it's a good thing because he got my bacon. I try to be really cool about it telling guys, because most guys are meat and potatoes kinda guys and I'm not some bimbo who only pretends to eat salads unless it has a wagon wheel of bread underneath it. #railhouserestaurant

#BODYSHAMING #SOCIALMEDIA

We all struggle with body shaming ourselves. But you know what? The size four you see at the gym has the same thoughts as the size 16 at the gym. We all have mommy stretch marks, we all have cellulite, we all eat leftovers off our kids plates and we all deserve a break. Unfollow anyone on social media who makes you feel like you aren't enough. Who has unrealistic goals for your body type and lifestyle. Wear the bikini! Enjoy your life the best you can, have grace.

Certain angles get you certain pic results. We choose good angles almost always. Which is ok. But when a bad angle is taken and your kid looks cute af in it, it's no longer about you. It's about her. So post that shiz.

Have you ever really struggled posting a photo of yourself because you look horrid? Me too. My beautiful daughter was coming off the softball field at a softball tournament and it took me a while to #justdoit. Why? Because I was in the background and you could see a lot of cellulite on my legs. The front/side of my thighs, my face was looking down, I looked frumpy. I didn't feel hot to trot. It took me about 20-30 minutes to talk myself into it. I tried cropping myself out, I tried making a cute scribble background around her head and body to omit my legs and face, and then I just did it. I said, you know what? It is what it is at this point. Get over yourself. This photo isn't about me, it's about her, and how proud of her I am, and how much of a softball player she has turned into. She hustles on the field, she hit a double today, and she is amazing, and not to mention the picture was just adorable with her little white hair and her smeared black eye marks. If I was to post the picture of her without myself in the background, would I kick myself later in life when the memory popped up and I would always remember that I was supposed to be in there with her? Would she want to see this picture later in life and remember when mom coached her softball team. Would she get the same body dysmorphia that I have because she will ask me later why it looks like that or who's legs and who's head is cut off.

On social media, we all post beautiful pictures of our kids and of ourselves. Never to see the flaws. I am guilty of it. Is it right? Is it wrong? I think we all just want to be the best versions of ourselves and it's hard when you think you look a certain way and then you see a photo and you are like "Whoaaa Buzz, your girlfriend" Getting dressed earlier that day I did struggle wearing shorts. My sports shorts from last year are tight, and they were even tight and short last year. I have thick thighs, so they always ride up. So I wore jean shorts that rode up, but not as bad, and I don't have a full length mirror, so looking down at my legs I saw muscle tone and I saw an opportunity to tan those white legs! I didn't see the cellulite that the camera captured. I didn't see the lumpy arm. I saw someone who was just trying not to die in this heat coaching nine little 7-9 year olds, on a field, with no trees or shade.

So I posted. Knowing that obviously people were going to see my legs and seriously think whoa gf has cellulite. So part of me was super embarrassed, and part of me was happy and confident that people can see a not so cute picture of myself and I was still ok (as ok as I was gonna be) posting it. Because that moment was about her, it wasn't about me. And my daughter was cute af and I was showcasing her. I thought about hashtagging mom legs, or something to make light of the situation I thought so many were going to see. But I didn't. I let them think what they wanted. They can say what they want and I will be ok with it. And you know what, I bet nobody fucking cared anyways, I was the only one thinking of how terrible my legs looked and I hope that by me posting that, they thought a little higher of themselves and won't be afraid to post a photo of them with their kids this summer. Because it's capturing the moment, making memories, and paving a path to the future. Post the picture.

#TACOHELL

I have been classified as obese as long as I can remember. Plain and simple. When I get my body fat/height/measurements bullshit taken, they say oh you are really flexible, have good balance, your waist and hip ratio is good, but when I calculate (beep bo beep bo) your height (beep bo) and weight, it's telling me that you are fffffff** fat. I was told that I am 136 lbs in muscle, and the rest is fat. I honestly was like yeah bro, boom, don't mess with the best and took that as a win, turns out it's not really a win. My BMI tells me I am obese Class 2. If I lost 25 lbs I would still be in obese Class 1. If I lost 55 lbs, I would STILL be classified as overweight. It goes Underweight, Normal Weight, Over Weight, Obese 1, Obese 2, Morbid. So what do I do?

I don't like those titles one bit. I don't think I deserve that title one bit. If the scale doesn't matter and it's just a "tool" then who the fuck keeps on telling doctors and fitness people to weigh people? How about you measure people in how many times you did something nice for someone this week. Or how many good friends you have. How many times you've sacrificed your sanity for your children's lives today. Today alone. If I had to change the BMI classification, I'd wager in tacos and burritos, there would be a measurement of 'how active are you' and that would offset your MORBID OBESITY in the BMI.

Underweight – Soft taco

Normal Weight – Soft Taco Supreme

Overweight – Bean Burrito

Obese 1 – Burrito Supreme

Obese 2 – Two Burrito Supreme's and a Mountain Dew.

Morbid Obese – Fourth Meal

And my questions would be: How much do you workout each day/week. Can you walk up the stairs without getting winded? Do you have one good friend who would call in sick to work to drink beer with you to cheer you up? Do you like your life? What are your top three goals in life? And somehow that would all calculate (beep bo beep bo) into each other and give you a life happiness number. You know, ask shit that matters. But for me, until I see a shrink, the scale will always somehow matter. As Weight Watchers is telling me I should lose a crap ton of weight (even though that's the program I have succeeded at in the past, cough cough, and fail at) Until I see a gaw damn rainbow emoji show up as my weight. And until I get into wONEderland, the scale is subconsciously my bitch, and I will fight. And I will continue to throw up numbers and squat your punk-ass ex girlfriend's weight.

#INCONCLUSION

I think I'm going to be ok. I'm where I'm at, and it has to be ok. I'm trying to lose, but not jumping on the scale much. I know 100% that in 10 or even five years, I will look back at myself and think, dang girl, why were you so hard on yourself? Why do you continue to hide your lady lumps? So a summer or two ago, I decided I am wearing ALL the swimsuits. You pet all the dogs, I'll wear all the suits. This is for those who think they aren't. Who think they can't. The only one stopping you, is you. One life, one try. Wear what you want and do what makes you happy, Eat what you want. Be Happy! Right now I'm simply trying to exist. If I eat a cheetoh I don't log it. Just trying to NOT be a nutbag…. As I sit here drinking wine out of a to-go coffee cup so my kids don't really know what I'm doing…. Is that a problem or a genius move? I am sure in one or two weeks, I'll have a bigger master plan, just being honest. If your pants don't fit you anymore, size up. Last summer I went into Walmart and got the biggest shorts I could get. There's no sense of feeling more sorry for yourself trying to fit into a pair of shorts from two years ago, especially in the summer heat that is called hell. I would take hot weather over snow anyday, so thank you Mother Nature for blessing Michigan. So what is my goal? Now that I am clearly on my way to stardom? My goal is to not binge. Get my shit together, eat like a 'real boy'. And maybe, just maybe in this process to find my sanity, be able to enjoy the finer things in life. Like wine in a coffee cup.

#GIRLFRIENDS

#NOHASHTAG

I don't have too much to say about girlfriends, because it's classified and sacred. Not really, but there's really no true bitching involved because my friends are the bees knees, legs and his arms. Such as Eminem raps in one of his songs. I mean, I grumble to them and move on. I then grumble about the same thing a few days later to them and then the next grumble is on that same topic, it eventually all fades, then comes back and we deal with it, again. Aahhh the circle of life. And they still love me. Always.

My girl gang is tight. My girl gang involves different ages, stages and races. Just kidding. We all little white girls. I live in a small town, so I can't help it. All my chicks provide me with different knowledge. If I'm having a rough day about men, I'll call one because texting just keeps me bottled up. And if she doesn't totally help me out, I'll call the next one, and then, if I still can't shake what I've heard or went though, I'll actually text my mom or dad, because they always help me even though I roll my eyes a lot. To have feelings and to express them and to NOT feel like a lunatic is the best. My friends and my parents do that for me. They side with me and make me feel loved. So thank you.

I have friends who have been with me since Elementary school and we don't skip a beat, and I have new adult friends that have come into my life the past five years. Who said being an adult and meeting new friends is hard? Just hang out at the same place and things happen. A strong friend foundation at our ages can simply be bonding over parenting, fitness, exes and just someone who you can relate to and trust. Trust is key.

#FRIENDDO'S

↔ Confess their love for me and tell me how much they miss me when it's been too long between hangs

↔ They let me vent whenever and about the same topic, until it's beaten and dead and beaten again

↔ They don't always say what I want to hear, because they are on the outside and see through clear eyes, not my foggy love tainted goggles

↔ They side with me and ask who's tires they need to slash at any given moment

↔ They are your rock when you can't function

↔ They love hearing your juicy gossip on boy stories and we drink wine and bum cigarettes from very questionable people at the bar

↔ One friend had me at "Lean Cuisines and Cigarettes"

↔ If there is a guy who keeps on breaking my spirit, she gets mad, we call him names, I swear him off, then he's back in my life and he asks me over and when I tell her, you would think she'd be mad, but she just says "well you obviously have to go right?"

↔ One lives in a bubble

↔ They get your so very stupid comments and usually response back with the same stupidity

↔ We start writing down the stupid thing we say in our phones and in a top secret notebook

↔ One was "the bitch' at work who turned out to be amazing

↔ We already decided we are having a joint plot at Riverside Cemetery

↔ They are gorgeous inside and out

#FAVORITEMEMORY

One of my favorite memories that gave me all of the feels.

"I've hit rock bottom," I said.

"Me too," she said without hesitation.

"I've been wearing the same sweats and sweatshirt for four nights," I told her.

"That's amazing," she said, as she stabbed her fifth piece of one week old, pre-cooked but frozen pizza and held it over the fire we started in my garage. It was a total smoke out.

You see, no matter what you are going through in life, someone else is going through it too. Your buds aren't always at rock bottom, at the same time you are, but when they are, there is no other way to go but up or sideways and you do it together. You check in with each other, you text, you hang out, you send funny memes, you tag each other on insta. You make plans to help each other. If you can truly have a couple of those in your backpocket, don't ever wash your jeans! Hrhrhrhr.

#LOVE

#LESSONSINLOVE

Your mind can be a b*tch. We are taught to be confident, kind, caring, compassionate, and forgiving at a very young age. But what about realistic? We aren't taught to be realistic. We are always told, shoot for the stars or you can be anything you want when you grow up.....etc. But what if what you want to be when you grow up is 'loved'. That's what I want, to be loved. By a partner. Not by my parents who love me unconditionally and not by my friends. I would hope that those two would be a given in most people's lives. Considering the type of person I have grown up to be with this damn Scarlett heart on my sleeve as it is. Loved by a worthy ass man.

It's been about week three of *Johnny Sucks A Lot* and I'm starting to see things from him that are opening my eyes.

1. I am not the one. 2. I will never be his one 3. Plain and simple.

But to truly get over this, I am honestly wondering if there is a 12 step thing. If there's not, I'll have to invent one.

The place that my mind has brought me to with the hopes and aspirations I have, all seem so childish right now. My heart throbs for someone who doesn't even think twice about me. How did this get so out of hand. Oh I know, I'm caring, kind and compassionate. The only way for me to actually move on and get over this is to completely cut myself off. Like 100% cut myself off. It's nearly impossible, with only myself only knowing the current situation with him. My closest friends don't even understand. I do believe everything happens for a reason, and sometimes it's not until a year or two later that things actually make sense. I wish that was the case right now. I'd love to fast forward and see why in the hell this man was brought into my life. Both parts of our lives, lined up, and continue to line up. It's really damn poetic and it's also very tragic. Let's put Johnny on the side for a second....

In the past 3 years, I've learned 3 things from 3 different guys.

#FIRSTLESSONINLOVE

The first one is quite profound and I do cherish this but the first guy's lesson was seriously put there to tell me that I am creating a sense of home for my kids. For example, the kids and I, we are home dwellers. We go to Nana's, GG's and have a pimp ass backyard and like having friends over. We don't have random cash laying around to just up and go outside the city limits on a whim when we are bored. We have a rainy day jar and that shit is planned. Hell, I can't even take them to Walmart for funsies without going over my budget, no way we can just spend a lovely day in Green Bay without me getting anxious of creating a fun day for free. So with cash frustration, at the end of my divorce, this man comforted me in telling me that I was the caregiver, the home maker. I was the one in charge of creating a home. A safe place, a memory spot. A feeling for them. That to me was very powerful and I am proud that I am able to do that for them. I now take leadership of creating a home very seriously.

Besides the sexual tension at first, as I look back now, he was never quite in it how I wanted him to be. He was always hesitant about everything. We never went in public, it was his house or mine, in public it was very straight laced because nobody knew.

#SECONDLESSONINLOVE

The second lesson I learned with dating recently was hell to the no to long distance. And hell no to a Farmer. They are dedicated to those cows. I get it. But I couldn't compete. It was about a 1.2 drive and I dreamed of eventually being his little milking lady with an apron on, as our kids were at school I'd look outside of the kitchen window and wave to him on the tractor. We were in the same boat divorce and kid wise, same schedule, and with my schedule switching weekends every four months, once my schedule put us off on opposite weekends, he threw in the towel. This was hard for me. So after I got over that a few months later, I realized I liked my nights *not* driving. When I get on Tinder now, I do still swipe on about 45+ miles, but only out of courtesy because if they are cute, I owe it to their mama to let them know her DNA is banging.

#THIRDLESSONINLOVE

And the third relationship was there as a reminder. As much as I want to tell you the bullet points, I'll leave it as he just reminded me a little of my ex and I felt like I was taking care of him, a 3rd child if you may. I do reach out to him off and on to check in, but the second I do, it reminds of why it didn't workout the first and second time. Lol.

Those were my staple lessons. Some more lessons were pretty straight forward and part of me knew the lesson before I even said hello, such as: no stoners, no Navy, and no married guys. ::sideways gallops:: kicks a couple rocks while whistling with my arms behind my back::

#THELASTLESSONBROKEME

Moving forward to reading the rest of this chapter, it's treacherous. It's a series of happy excitement, then let-downs. Repetitiveness that took me almost a year to catch on to. Well ok, maybe nine months, then it took me six months to cut it off. A relationship that started as friends, then went further in only my head and heart. The patterns of let's hang out, let's be friends, how can I help, stop at my house, and then a week or two later, vanish, got old. Grab a pack of cigarettes then take a seat.

#WEMEET #JOHNNY

I've seen him before, a couple times. I'm always amazed at how people I have never seen before, just come into my path. I've lived in the same city my whole life. Minus college and a few stints in Green Bay. I guess 10,000 people is a lot after all. Johnny was dripping with sweat, coming in to kiss his daughter at practice, so fast, a kiss on the lips, thinking how sweet. Months later, I introduced myself over plate weights and earbuds. You can tell a lot about a person's handshake, and he had it. I reached out, we met thumb web to thumb web, not afraid to really dive in.... Our handshake was solid and strong, his eyes were soft and his smile was perfect, and I knew it was over. So much confidence, his whole aura, his existence, but that smile.... And he seemed humble. I am a pretty good judge of character.

#SUNSHINE

Two whole weeks of morning and night snaps/text. Two whole weeks. Pictures, alarm clocks, coffee, boots, bikes, eye rolling emojis and selfies. Two whole weeks, of the beginning of my shot, my chance at a real relationship with him. Was it really going to happen this time? Did he really choose me? I hate to be negative about this and pessimistic, so I jumped in full force. Let's do this! The day he left for the road we had a snap streak flame going. But as the hours went past, his stories got longer and longer, and our flame lost it's intensity by the hour, and the next day of no picture snaps, it was gone. My two week excitement was only to be broken with miles of distance. Subconsciously all along, I knew he would miss her and not me, and after his final destination, he would turn around and go back to her.

#ILLUSIONS

The truth is, this man I dream of often does not exist. He was in parts of my life, but where my mind and heart go is one sided. I cry writing this because I wanted it so bad. It's all an illusion that sometimes still seems like if I just reach my arm out, just enough, he'll grab my forearm and pull me into him. Put his other arm on the small of my back and hold tight. Tell me it's always been me and he's fought it for so long. It's unrealistic. For someone to mean so much to me and the other side of the relationship is non-existent. On a daily basis, my heart got broken, over and over. What keeps me going is hope, but it's also what crushed my soul. When I think of this relationship I've quite possibly made it up in my head, I'm also quite possibly in love.

#RACHELHOLLIS

Chapter five is where I lost it in *Girl Wash Your Face*. Because I, too, fell the first time I saw him. I'll never forget that morning. Her words in Chapter 5, resonate with me, her explanation. I knew it all too well. In my past two years I always feel like I've always been the booty call in a lot of relationships. Keep up, because my heart jumps and beats fast when it comes to feelings.

Loving him is enough for me. Rachel talks about the moment she saw him and started a relationship, which turns out to be one of those and I quote her "I'm not with him, but I'm not not with him" kind of relationship.

The initial first date, the flirty texts, the mixed signals, waiting for the text, the games that inflate my heart to max capacity. The mind games, I'm not going to text him first, but then I always cave in, because damn it, I'm in my 30's and don't have time or patience for games.

After a year of Rachel's *Girl Wash Your Face* up and down relationship. They were together, but not together, the booty calls, the mixed signals in front of friends. She opened her eyes to the fact that she was hanging onto the thought of love - not actual love. She explained it as being stuck or lost in a forest and not being able to see the trees. For me, I want that physical connection so bad, I pretend to be ok not seeing the trees. Guys want the chase, and I am good about it for like three days. Then I am like 'ok, what's up. So we gonna do this or what?'

I'm not talking like 'in a relationship' on Facebook so fast, but, not like three days without talking. How do people go from texting off and on all day, to zero. I would at least like to know.

They say "I'm so sorry, I've just been really busy." Really? Such a little boy lie.

Loving him is enough for me. So what does that mean? It's ok for love to be one sided? I love him, I'll do all the work, I'll try my hardest to make him happy and in return be ok getting not much in return. I use the word love, not because it's true love, or "I Love You's" are exchanged, but because it's the whole package, the chase, the fall, the heartbreak, the butterflies. Even if it doesn't develop into anything, we most definitely learn how we want to be treated and how we deserve to be treated in that short period of time.

(Johnny) Inviting me up to the roof for flirty banter. Complimenting me by telling me he liked my *demeanor*. One of the most prestigious compliments I've ever gotten, as it's unique and original. How would my head not spin, how would I not wonder. The "I like how we are." comments. "I like coming over to your house and building things." But probably not in the way I, myself, like how we are.

So, do I, like Rachel, accept that "loving him is enough for me."

I am only good enough for him when he is not with anyone else. And I truly understand that. If I had a guy, I wouldn't hang out with him or text him as much, because I'd have someone else to take up my time. As Rachel wraps up her relationship that 'just good enough' she says, and I even highlighted it in the book.

"I am done with this. I am done with you. Don't ever call me again." She explained, "It wasn't a bid for attention, or an attempt at playing hard to get: I meant every single word."

"Why?" He choked.

"Because I don't deserve to be treated like this. Because I can't go back and forth. Because I don't like what I've become...but mostly because you said we were friends. This whole time, whatever else has happened, you told me I was your friend. I don't want to be friends if this is how you treat someone you care about" Rachel said.

So as I sit here thinking of the guy, I hold on a pedestal, how do you cut the rope with someone who you have too many ties to. Even though he is helpful whenever I need it. Even though "I never bother him," "I like you company," "I'm on my way to your house," "I'm packing my bags," "I fell for the girl who had the organized chalkboard wall." These are all things Johnny has said to me. I'm beginning to think, loving him..... is not..... enough for me......

#DOINGGIRLFRIENDTHINGS

"So am I going to help you or not turd?" I texted him after waiting for a month to hear from him.

"Yes." He said. "Do you have the kiddos?"

"No" I said.

"Do you want to come over tonight?

"Sure" my heart pounded.

"Should I cook, I mean, I have to feed my daughter."

"Sure" Heart pounding.

Still taken away and scrunching my eyes and nose as if Ashton Kutcher was going to pop out and tell me I was getting punked.

So we hung out for about three hours. I can never seem to get enough. Dinner, dishes, trampoline, hot tub, work stuff, hug, home. He didn't say goodbye, he never does, but I left happy knowing that he could have hung out with anyone and he chose to hang out with me. I even got to wear his sweatshirt and really wanted to wear it home, but I didn't want to be *'that girl'* But maybe that's what he wants. That girl. The girl who squeals, the girl who nestles her toes under his butt on the couch and complains she's cold. Maybe he wanted someone he could take care of. I'm just so used to taking care of people, that I don't feel comfortable yet to be 'that girl'.

I felt like he looked at me differently that night. It was like the look of happiness, calmness and safety? Is that a thing? Almost as if I was to lean in, he may reciprocate. But I couldn't risk it. I couldn't break my ego like that if he stopped me. He clearly has major hesitations when it comes to me. Like, sometimes I feel like we were connecting on a different level, and then the next it's just useless conversation and I am not even sure he sees me or realizes it's me talking to him. I noticed that today. He always always, is in a good mood. I have never once seen him crabby or quiet. I have snapped at him multiple times with my hormones and crabbiness, and he always has his shit together. Almost too much.

Like he is hiding something. Like if he was to be vulnerable and show himself, he would fall apart or lose his manhood. I snap, he tells me to relax, and doesn't hold it against me.

And after just one night of hanging out together, I already knew I needed to make a decision. All or nothing. No grey. I guess it was my turn to actually ruin the friendship. If it was my looks and he wasn't attracted, then I guess there's nothing I can do about it.

I called my girlfriend the next day after being in a fog for hours contemplating 100% sabotage to sew up my bleeding heart.

"What do I do?" I said.

"Well what do you want to do?" She asked.

"I don't know, it's really hard."

"I know it is."

"I think I need to end it all." I said crying now. "I feel better without him. Without wondering if he's going to text me or wondering when he'll be single again and want to be my friend again." I sobbed.

"Well, it looks like you found your answer" She said slowly.

And just like that my mind was made up. I was going to write him a love letter, mail it and be done.

"Pour it all out" She said.

"I will."

And instantly I felt relieved, knowing that in that moment of our relationship, I was in charge of my feelings and had to handle them.

#THELETTERINEVERSENT

I am handsdown 100% in love with you. I have been the moment we shook hands. I knew I was screwed from the second we met. It's been a little over two years, building this relationship and I can't do it anymore. I can't pretend to be ok not talking to you every day. I can't pretend not to care when you keep choosing 'her' over me. And I'm sure as hell done pretending I'm ok without talking to you for months. You want friendships and relationships with people who have other common grounds than you, well here I fucking am. My list is endless with you. This is your chance, and you are throwing it all away. You don't want to ruin our friendship by dating me. For the sake of my heart, I guess I'll have to. I want nothing but happiness and success for you in your career and your life. I want it as bad as I want you. I just want to be with you. And you can't do that, so I can't do this.

♥ - Allyson

Day Dreaming:: The leaves were twirling and dancing with each other the day I walked to the mailbox on the corner. Like little kids giggling on the playground. My hands were cold and my nose was running. As I held the little blue handle open, I pressed the turquoise envelope on my nose and lips, kissed the seal, and walked away.

#NOWAYDIDTHISJUSTHAPPEN

He texted me from the roof. He was working while I was working. It was weird and kinda cool. So I climbed the ladder up to chat with him. You could see everything from up there. We had some small talk and a little flirting I guess. He was caulking a portion of the roof and couldn't get it out and said "oh great, I'm trying to be all smooth working with this gun and it is not working."

I didn't even realize he was trying to be smooth. I mentioned to him that I was getting a half sleeve-ish that night and he seemed super interested. He asked what time, what I was getting and he said he wanted to stop in and see it. He wanted to stop at the place… to see me…. getting a tattoo….. this was big. So I was like *yeah sure*, told him what time and he was like *ok cool*. The plans of him wanting to see me ended our conversation at a good point. I felt I could get off the rooftop. I asked him if he wanted me to take the ladder with me so he didn't have to put it away, he smirked and declined my offer.

Later that night, as I sat in the chair, squinching my butt cheeks and grinding my teeth, a text came in, from him. Fucking fuck. He really wanted to come here! I honestly thought he was just being kind earlier in the day. Wut is going on. Who is this guy? Why am I so cool to hang out with all of a sudden? It was the calmest feeling I've had from him in a while, from the second I saw his text until the time of me reading it, everything seemed to go in slow motion.

He ended up getting caught up in something, but this was all blowing my mind. Even though we were friends, I was just like oh my gosh, it's happening. Even after missing me at the shop, he still wanted to come over. I offered him a Squagle to eat. It's an old trick I learned in high school from my friend Heather. Bagel + Cheese = Squagle. Like Queso and cheese and bagel. It's deep, I know. That's all I could offer him, not only because I was internally freaking out, but because I only had condiments or frozen pizza and I knew he wouldn't go for that especially after his processed cheese comment. (Just eat the freaking cheese) We ended up at Menards that night and he helped me put together a bookshelf. I wondered if people thought we were together walking around together. He said he didn't like having a girlfriend during Christmas, so he usually breaks it off a little before that. What a little flirt. I don't comment much when he flirts, because about a year ago I told him to cut the crap with me and to not flirt with me. Ever. But I mean, who couldn't flirt with this slice of pie?

So even though I could get the attention of other men, I didn't want them. I wanted him. Still after all the letdowns. The other guys were just distractions and ego boosts. It's not real, it's lust. I never even wanted his body, I wanted his heart, his mind, his soul. And until I get that or find someone who replaces you, you will all be fillers.

#THEBRIGHTESTLANTERN

I was painting my nails the second night he stopped over that week. I asked him red or blue and he chose blue. He sat down on the couch and I was on the Chaise. Sweats, tank top, high ponytail. He was wearing a sweatshirt and sweats and looked damn perfect. I don't know if he does this to a lot of people, but he bared his soul that night. Told me everything. His childhood, his teens, his current situations now. And I felt so deeply hurt for him that I almost crawled across the carpet to give him a hug. I don't know why I can't move to hug him when I want to, but I just can't in fear that he will stiff arm me. So I didn't crawl across the carpet. I listened, I shook my head alot and I was just there for him. Man, I wish I would have given him a hug, even when he left. Just hugged him. Tell him how brave he is, how awesome his story is. But I just couldn't. I never want to make him feel uncomfortable. It's that deep respect I have for him. I felt honored and closer to him on another level that night. So he left, and I couldn't stop thinking about him and the beautiful story he told me.

I sent him this quote before bed and I meant every word of it.

"I look at you and see all the ways a soul can bruise, and I wish I could sink my hands into your flesh and light lanterns along your spine so you know there is nothing but light when I see you." Shinji Moon

That is the kind of connection I felt to him that night. Soul shaking, chanting voodoo, moon praising respect.

#ISTHISREAL

1.5 hours in a hot tub. I wanted nothing more than to swim over to him and lay myself on top of him. And just hold him, hug him, feel his warm body, his tight embrace. Feel his neck wrap around mine. I just want to feel the electricity that keeps our fuses burning. Then he slowly moves his neck from mine, grazing my cheek with his lips, slowly, my heart is pounding, my arms go limp at the mere thought of what may happen next. The corner of our lips touch and I can't help but to lock them together. Lock them with the sweetest most innocent kiss. A kiss that tells him, 'YES dammit, it's me, it's always been me" My eyes are closed as a tear runs down my face and I know he feels it, because he grabs my jawline and kisses my cheek, then goes into my lips for another kiss. My top lip is over his, for the longest, but shortest five seconds of my life. The best five seconds of my life is over.

We continued our conversation of paper rock scissors and Thanksgiving rituals. He shows me a picture of his mother from one conversation. Each time we hang out, I get more information, but I still hold back sharing myself, knowing, he will soon be gone. I try not to ask too many questions even though I want to know everything about his life. Everything. He is so beautiful on so many levels and I want to tell him that. I want to wrap my arms around him and tell him that he is perfect on every level, and I accept his past and I want his future but mostly I want his scars. I want us to lay on his bed side by side with our wet swimsuits on as I trail my fingers down on his back muscles, leaning in closer to kiss. As I leave his house, he wraps my scarf around my neck, takes my hand and leads me to the door. But as he kisses my forehead and tells me he'll talk to me later, I know it's a lie. He doesn't call and he didn't plan on calling, and I knew it the second those words left his beautiful lips.

#OFFGUARD

He was single again. I haven't had contact with him in over a month and he seemed to reach out to me more than normal last night. Maybe he was just searching for a familiar face in a crowded room, but he makes me so nervous. I clam up, I make weird comments, I shorten the conversations or make an excuse to leave. But last night he kept coming to me.

Time stood still as I saw him coming through the doors. No matter how pissed or hurt or confused I was by him, I am never truly mean in person to him nor do I say what I'm really feeling. At least I think I'm smiling ear to ear whenever I see him, even though my eyes throw daggers. It's just a habit to be as positive as I can around him. I was so stressed out yesterday, so crabby and I fought hard to prevay that attitude towards him, but I failed. Because he honestly brings out the best in me. He makes me want to (gag) be a better person, think about the positive things and he makes me happy. He came downstairs to see me.

He said this in slow motion I swear, "I just wanted to see if you needed any help."

I was pretty annoyed with that comment, with him coming in five minutes of *go time* to see if I needed any help.

One of the volunteers must have sensed our chemistry and commented, "Ohhh is that your husband?" I bit my tongue so hard and tried not to say anything cocky.

"So we don't see each other for a few weeks and you just off and go and get married," Johnny said. "Well congratulations."

Well that was just fucking awkward for me. Really? He had to pretend I got married and dodge the whole topic that she thought *WE* were married. Awesome. It sucks for me that he pays so much attention to details, lets me know he keeps track of time, or things that are said. So here I go obsessing about it. I was pissed that night, but felt confident at the same time because he was seeking me out.

I had the night all mapped out and my plan didn't even last 10 minutes. I'd see him, say hello and shoot small impersonal banter and then I wouldn't make contact with him the rest of the night. Boom, Bam, Simple. Well, in all actuality, I had more than one encounter with him that night. Damn. It. Mission. Denied. It was him like all night. He shot laser beams at me so I could sense where he was the whole night. Fucker. About 15 minutes into the night I had to make an announcement so I made my way across the dance floor by him in passing and he scooted his butt quickly towards me to block my path and I swatted his ass. I didn't see the side step happening, so I did what any normal person would do and slap his ass. (squinching my eyes and pondering life at this moment) Why, when I close the door, lock the box, throw away the key, he's there banging on it. Every fucking time.

I don't want to fall for him anymore than I already have. I already know what I feel. But I can only imagine what I would feel like if I dropped my guard and became one of his groupies. On a few occasions that I've had to pry out of him, he's mentioned to me he isn't into me more than a friend. So after the 3rd time of hearing this rejection, which I needed, my walls started to get sturdier and taller, yet kind of wimpy, like the little pig who built his house out of sticks. It wants to be strong, but so is not. An oxymoron if you may. Sometimes mixed signals fall out of the cracks which creates a second guessing lady out of me. If a tiny squirrel grabbed a stick from my wall, I'd be so screwed. Well, the little squirrel interacted again with me again. He smiled the whole time, ear to ear. He mentioned his daughter liked when I gave him crap. So immediately I thought in my head, ahhh she sees the chemistry too. Just like all of fucking A-merica. Does she know the actual level of our communication? Does anyone even know the level of our relationship? This whole time we talked, I didn't notice anyone else in the room because of his aura. Do you know those movies where the room goes in slow motion and the people walk in slow motion to each other, it's like that. My life does that when he is around. His presence, his core.

Later that night I awkwardly I opened a package of napkins and began to wipe up the floor by him. Naturally, as I was down there, I shined his shoe and told him he owed me a quarter. He reached into his pocket and pulled out lint and a plaquer. I declined the offer and we both laughed. Later kicking myself, how awesome would it have been to put that plaquer in my mouth, salute him with 2 fingers and walk off.....

#LUCIDDREAM

"Will you kiss me, just to see if I feel anything?" I asked him in the hottub that cold November night. "And if I do feel something, and you don't, I will leave right away."

He didn't say anything so I inched closer through the water. I was so scared. Scared that as I was moving closer to him, he would realize what is about to happen and stop me. I glided toward him until my hands were on each of his thighs and my legs were floating underwater behind me. I softly grabbed his top lip with mine and pushed in.

That was all that I needed to know, I had to leave. As I unlocked our lips, I looked down as tears started to stream down my face and I walked to get my towel. In my mind, he grabbed my hand and pulled me back in. But in reality, I went home that night, alone. The most electric kiss of my life, and it was over.

#CATFIGHT

I was wrong about everything. He's not over there obsessing or event thinking about our next encounter. Something is wrong and something has changed. How does one person go from saying *"put me on your favorites call list"* and now acting as if I'm non-existent. Do you think it's his girlfriend? She has a sixth sense and knows something is or was up. I mean duh, that's why she unfriended me.

When you unfriend someone, you are usually looking for a source of empowerment or ego boost because you are jealous, intimidated, hurt and just want to feel superior. Does she also give him a gnarly look when he talks to me? Last time that happened to me was when I was in college and I was into my best friend. Well, well, history is repeating itself. When I graduated and left the town one of my so-called friends, swooped right in on my college man. She also made up some bogus story to him that I had said some stupid shit to her and he wasn't allowed to talk to me. Do girls really do that still?

I knew I would put a target on my back the second I wrote on his wall and I was up for the challenge. I don't want to be a secret anymore. I wanted people to know we had a really cool whatevership. As he once asked me "why do I attract the syko's." Was he trapped? Was he too good of a guy to say no and break her heart? I I don't understand how people can break up and make up so many times. I just don't. She had to be his kryptonite. If I wrote him 'are you ok?' Right now-what would his response be? I can picture him taking his phone into the bathroom and pretend to poop, just so he can respond. I just wanted to know what he was feeling. I always want to know how he is doing. I want him to come over and tell me his life story. I wanted my friend back.

#SPEEDDIAL

I texted him one morning after I locked my keys in my car. This was the day after the first time, I broke everything off with him the night before. Friendship, flirting, hanging out, whatever we were or weren't, I broke it off. I know, I really took the bull by the horns, only to be awoken the next day to reality that I needed him, he is my blankey. He is my life preserver. He calms me. Puts reason in my head.

He responded with "What do you need me to do to help you," "Do you need a car?" "Do you need me to bring you somewhere?"

I felt helpless and I don't like asking for help, especially after I made a stink the night before saying I can't even be friends with him. A part of me knew I messed up and God was putting him back in my life. Yeah, we'll go with that. I ended up in my head too much and told him I would just figure it out. 2 hours later I called him so he could hear the pain/hurt/love/frustration/thankfulness in my voice, and I was in tears. Explaining I am so sorry I always run to him, but he is the first person I think to call when I need help and I hate it and it's not fair.

The first thing he replied with was that we can still be friends. I'd like to think that what I told him the night before got to him a little and stung. Making him wonder if he messed up, or if he didn't want to lose me yet. (I got the sense that he wasn't being a dick by saying 'friends' like platonic, but friends like, friends. Friends who see the ugly, friends who see the good, friends who are there) I sobbed that I knew we could, but it sucks for me because I will always want more. So what do you do, when you are infatuated with your best guy friend? A friend, who is just that.

He comes and goes in my mind, some weeks are better than others not thinking about him. But I could almost contact him everyday if I wanted to about something. Excuses. Excuses to ask for help, to see him or hang out. But I refrain, knowing, I'm the one getting hurt, not him. Knowing that the more I know, the more I grip on, the more I need to let go of in the end. So what do you do when after all the crazy, all the stupid things you have said or asked him about, he still tells you to put him on speed dial, have him named #1 in his phone. How does that not give a girl hope? Am I crazy. Is this all worth it?

#CONFUSION

I woke up feeling sad but only because my heart knows what it needs to do, I am still mixed with emotion from last night's dreams. He was in my dream last night. It wasn't vivid, it was a distant dream where I could just recall bits and pieces and truly only saw him in a fog. All I remember when I woke up was him saying that 'if I can handle that, then he's in' Was he was 'breaking-up' with me?, But as a friend? Nobody puts baby in the corner! Or was he solidifying yet again, in another lump of crap words, that he's just not that into me. Is it worth it, to keep someone around, who yes, is amazing, but is hot and cold. He physically is replaceable. But I'm not sure how those eyes and smile will ever be filled again. It scares me to cut ties with someone I've built the best kind of relationship with. So right now, as bad as it hurts, as bad as I want to just reach out and stop playing games with myself.

I need to just disconnect. Be so deep into myself that no one else matters, except for those who really want to be in my life. Those who text or call and reach out. Those who make plans with me, or comment on my shenanigans. As hard as it is, this is it. I deserved to be friends with someone who knows the meaning of friendship. Someone who doesn't just fill the air with words or generic flirty comments to keep me close. Sometimes, there is a general blankness in his cheap comments that make me feel like a number. As bitchy as that is for me to say, I really don't know what to think anymore. The way I feel for him and what he reciprocates makes me feel easily replaceable and kind of dirty. So he wins, I have to let myself be replaced by another. Push him into her arms. But I'll tell you what, I am not replaceable. I'm not about to wait around when he realizes, I was a rare tulip, and all those other girls were pansies.

#THEWHATEVERSHIPBREAKUP

It went down for about 24 hours. Most of the conflict was inside myself and has been for a while, but the final straw was I realized, he did not trust me 110% with his life. If I give you everything I have, my trust, my vulnerability, my time and my heart over and over, you would think he saw my loyalty. I have been nothing but honest and open and trustworthy to this man and he didn't see it. At least his actions and words used, proved to me that if I was on the edge of a cliff, about to fall to my death, I could see him just watching me, because he was hesitant to let me in and keep me close.

So for 24 hours I questioned a lot. Why I continued to associate myself with someone who doesn't fucking have a clue. As much as I pretend to not care and not think. I care. I think. When you just aren't close to someone you thought you were, it makes you question your confidence in that relationship. So I had to move forward without him. Starting. Right. Moew.

That was the final straw, I've tried to get out of our friendship a few times, not because I didn't think he was amazing. Because he was. I finally had enough... feeling like I wasn't enough. Nothing I did was ever good enough, I was never pretty enough, I was never skinny enough, I was never sober enough. And those insecurities were my own and they were ugly, and I was denied enough by him that I started to believe he thought those things my head continued to tell me. Today, I'm single, let's hang out and text for a few days, then one week later, there is no contact and I get one word answers and "I'm busy."

I was just done. I can't exactly go into detail what I did - but it made me question the way I thought he saw me and felt about me as a whole person. He would argue nothing bad happened and that I misunderstood. And I would argue that he didn't treat me with respect and kindness, treating me like someone he had just met. He would argue I blew it up or out of proportion. #bomb #boom #youcantsaybombonanairplane

I came out fighting with passion of course in the final texts that would conclude our whatevership. It all happened pretty fast. Like a 100 yard dash. Usually the world slows down when I talk to him, but this time my heart was racing and it wouldn't slow down. I was on edge, when he texted back, oddly his responses were fast, I slowly closed my eyes and started to slowly put my phone to my chest, then my phone went off again, and my heart jumped, then it went off again, oh shit, is he pissed? The fact that he was mad, meant I meant something right? I ignited something and damn it, tells me I'm not crazy. I skimmed his words I didn't want to read and I didn't understand what he was trying to say because his points were invalid to me. I refused to let anything he said persuade me to believe anything else than what I had ultimately felt for 24 hours straight.

Pure adrenaline and hell. I read the texts, and at this point I felt the need to throw in an f bomb. He asked me to please relax and that he would call me when he got a break. I dodged the suggestion of a phone conversation because I knew that somehow he would get me back. I told him he didn't need me and to not make it hard for me. He tried to explain to me again, in some way that he still needed me and at this point it was too late for me. I told him I was replaceable. Because for two years he's shown me nothing but that. The thing he will never admit is that he needed me because he did care about me on some other level.

"It's because I fucking care, when you care about something it shows, so find someone who cares, that's all you need to do. This isn't a war, get back to work, I didn't want this to be an argument or a debate" I said to him.

"Ok" he said.

That is all he said. Ok.

And that my friends, is how you end it. Months of ups and downs. Of being so excited of the unknown and the butterflies of hanging out and then let down about a week later, about three different times months apart. I knew I was done when last month I made myself hold a straight face when I saw he messaged me. I had a straight face and had to be cool if I spoke about him. Even though I'm sure my eyes had hearts in them like a cartoon character. But that's when I knew, it wasn't about him anymore, it was about me. I've become a watered down version of myself because there was no joy, it wasn't exciting, it was a constant let down. Constant, for nine months. (Until I had our baby. Hahaha plot twist, no I'm kidding.) I was his backburner girlfriend. He was keeping me around 'in case' down the road, he wanted something to happen. So I took a bow, and I had to be mean about it.

#PEACE

How did I know I was doing the right thing? I knew I was doing the right thing when I felt a sense of pressure release off my heart. Like I knew I was going to heal. I've healed before, and I know it would happen again, but I needed to stop the communication, I needed to stop the 'what ifs' and 'waiting game.' Cutting off ties to him made me feel powerful for about three hours until it made me sad.

For a while it felt like I was losing out. Like I was weak for not being able to remain friends. Why was I holding onto someone who didn't make me feel sexy or wanted? Why did I do that? Trying to wear a different swimsuit everytime we hot-tubbed. It took me so long to realize my worth because I struggled with only having him as a friend and still wanting more. When my girlfriends were sending me cute and meaningful memes, my heart smiled, but then I was like oh poor me. Like what the F. I am sexy. I am fierce. I am fun. I don't need to feel bad because one guy chooses to not choose me.

I think I finally got to this point because deep down I did know where he stood. I knew he wasn't interested by the way he told me, more than once. I needed him to tell me exactly why. But you become this robot when you aren't able to be yourself. You can't flirt how you usually do, because you know it's a platonic relationship. You can't say inappropriate things because you don't want to scare them off because they know you care. It's not like your buddy from 4th grade who you feel so comfortable with he's your brother. It's not like that. You think it's like that because you crave some sort of connection with them, but from the outside looking in, you aren't being your fun flirty spontaneous self, you are guarded. And each day that you have to pretend to not care, is another day you are further from yourself. You don't realize it because you are in too deep. Man, I am like blowing my own mind right now.

I was dulling myself down to fit into his world. I was making excuses. I wouldn't say what I was feeling, I held back. I wasn't completely ridiculous like I usually am.

And you know how I knew? An old, well I can't even call it a flame, but an old flame that meant absolutely nothing to me from the past, we played softball against eachother maybe ONE game and flirted. He added me to facebook. And I was excited. I was like wow, out of the blue, and I felt an instant connection to him, because of those times I taunted him on 1st base. It was instant fire. Instant feels. I wasn't anxious because the physical attraction and connection was felt both ways. Do you know what it's like to wait for a text from someone who doesn't quite share the connection that you want for 30 minutes? Imagine waiting for a day, or an hour for a text message. It's pure hell. Waiting should be an emotion. It's anxiety, excitement, sadness, happiness, disappointment and relief all rolled into one. It's the worst emotion of them all because it's a rollercoaster. And at some point, we all need to get off that roller coaster. Some of us never return, and some of us always return to it. ::Exits roller coaster and pukes into a garbage can::

#SNAPCHAT

I wondered if his snaps were for me to see this weekend? Like subconsciously he wanted me to miss him and reach out. He wished we would cross paths. The way that I wish every weekend, he felt it. But I know better. He's a dude they're simple. Deep down I hoped he wished I was sitting next to him, he wished I was next to him in the car, he wished I was laying on the pillow next to him. My hand reaches for my phone and almost texts him weekly. Each time I see his name pop up on the storyline this weekend my heart skips a beat and the anxiety of feelings rush back. I kept his selfie up as long as I could until my phone dimmed. At one point my fingers reached for the screenshot buttons but, no one likes a stalker. His snaps just reminded me of how bad I still miss him.

If I could just stay in the angry stage forever. Where it just feels better. It feels better to drink massive amounts of haterade and just hate. Anger. Dismissal. When I'm not seeing him or thinking about him because we just don't have contact anymore, I am completely fine. But one earshot of his name, or flash of social media, I just melt. I die a little, knowing it'll never be me.

It's always a slap in the face when someone still suggests I date him. Like yes Karen, I know we would make a killer couple.

#MONTHSGOBY

I miss you like crazy. I miss your energy. I miss your emoji eyerolls. I miss your truck rolling through my alley. So many people around me need you. You are prestigious. Just reading your name cracks my heart and slows my mind. It brings me back to when you stopped over with your cousin just to say hi, and proceeded to tell me that you told him that you liked my company. It took me back to the time we were talking on the phone and you called me your best friend and we both laughed in agreement. That week that we were 'best friends' was one of the best. You snapped me every morning and on and off all day. After that, you said you would change my name in your phone. I was always curious to see if you actually did and what it was. I get mad now thinking about how happy I was after that conversation.

Now, I cringe at the thought of seeing you in public. It's been months of nothing. Silence. Both ends. I've thought about what would happen when I finally do see you and it could go three different ways.

1. It could go like we never skipped a beat and I fall back into your web. But however it goes you initiate, I feed off your first reaction. We don't skip a beat, you come up to me and give me a high five or a stupid pound, say something stupid, and I quietly smirk at you as you talk, admiring you as if you are a painting in the Gugenheim. I want to reach out and touch you so bad, feel your arm, touch your face. Make sure it's real.

2. Or it could go tragically where I quietly say hi, awkwardly smile with my lips closed, I wave small like an idiot and we keep moving along. You don't even acknowledge me, and I don't know why and I never ask.

3. Or my best version yet, would be tragic. We see each other and the world stops. We say nothing and walk to each other and hug hard. It doesn't feel weird. I kind of rub my hands on your back and shoulders. I slightly turn my head towards your jaw making contact with your neck and my breath. It's innocent, but it means more this time. There's something in the hug that makes me believe you actually miss me. You smell like your house and it brings me back to the time I forgot my vest there. When I picked it up and wore it, the smell of your house kept for a week. I wanted the smell to stay, but I also needed it to leave. So after our hug, you look me in the eyes and they start to tear up, which makes mine tear up. You kiss my forehead, move your hands down my arms and for a second we hold fingers, then you brush past me. No words. None.

#TAYLORSWIFT

"And I just want to tell you, that it takes everything in me, not to call you. And I wish I could run to you, I hope you know that everytime I don't, I almost do. I hope, sometimes you wonder about me. I bet it never, ever occured to you, that I can't say hello to you and risk another goodbye."

I Almost Do - Red Album

#DEBBIEDOWNER

In the end, I always lose. I always lose. I try so hard to be happy and pretend to be ok, living for my kids, my friends and my family. When really, all I want is someone to love me beyond words. They say I haven't found my person yet. I'm beginning to think maybe my person is actually just me. Which would be such a waste to not have all of this love oozing out of my soul - that is bursting inside of me. To not share that passion of life with anyone, would be so sad to me.

I seem to always be that pivotal girl. The girl in between a breakup or the one when they are lonely and want to talk. Everything I ever felt or thought I knew about love, is shit. It's complete shit and it sucks.

#MYWISHFORLOVE

"If you want something to last forever, you treat it differently. You shield it and protect it. You never abuse it. You don't expose it to the elements, you don't make it common or ordinary. If it ever becomes tarnished, you lovingly polish it until it gleams like new. It becomes special because you have made it so, and it grows more beautiful and precious as time goes by." *F. Burton Howard*

#THEHONESTTRUTH

Here is the truth. You deserve everything. You don't have to settle for anything. There is always someone out there who is going to think the world of you. Someone who is going to do whatever they need to do to make you happy and keep you happy. I know this because I was that person. And I know that because in a weird way, I had that at one point, it was just the wrong kind of love. The love that you keep going back to because it's all you know, but you know, deep down, there is an even better love, one that is healthy. Someone is going to look at you and think damn, I'm lucky. Someone who is going to drop everything they are doing to come and rescue you from whatever dilemma you got yourself into. Someone who is going to want nothing but butterflies and rainbows for your life, and they want to be there every step of the way to make sure those butterflies don't die and the rainbow doesn't fade. They will see the good in you when you don't see it.

And if you are looking for that in someone who isn't capable of giving that to you, then try every single day to move on. Cut whatever strings need to be cut and call it what it is. His loss. Baby girl, you deserve the ring, you deserve the house, you deserve the memories. You deserve the life you've always wanted. Sure, everything gets sticky. Although I am hurt, or have been hurt, I know that in my heart someone will want those things for me. And if it takes me putting myself out there and letting go of people who don't see my value, even though I value them so much. I have to question my motives. Why? Why am I settling or hoping or wishing for something to come true that just isn't meant to be.

You can't change anyone, and morphing yourself into a watered down version of yourself is Luda. Why would you? Be 100 proof. If you can't come in hot with a side bun, wispies falling down in front of your face, shoes half way on and 3 bags slung on your shoulders and still feel beautiful....then you need to check it. Some of the days where I feel the most beautiful and comfortable in my skin are those days. Those days I'm coming in hot and I have a purpose to every movement I make and being on point with my hair or clothes isn't something I even have time to think about. I am not one to match everyday, I am simply doing the damn thing and owning who I am.

This is me. I can be loud, I laugh with my whole body, I joke around, my filter is broken with almost everyone to an extent and for the most part I feel and give with my whole heart. And if there is someone who won't take that beautiful big heart of yours and keep it whole, and want to keep your rainbow colorful and butterflies alive with every inch of their being, then you have to move on. If you give them chance after chance to make them try to understand how your heart beats for them, and they push it aside not seeing your original beauty, then guess what, choose yourself. If you have five good people in your life, who you know will drop anything to help you or take you out on the town when you need to just dance, or someone who will just sit and listen and give advice, even if it's the same things they say over and over to you. Then you my friend, you already have it all. Wait for the one who will give you what that other schmuck isn't able to. It doesn't mean he's a bad guy, it just means, he isn't your guy.

We are humans, we have feelings. If you feel like you are just a number in their book, allow yourself to erase your number. Move on. Don't be the backburner.

#DATING

So people off and on say to me, oh just stop looking and poof someone will come into your life. But then people also say, why don't you put yourself out there more. Take the risk, go out and meet people. Ok Karen, what is it, do I go out and get rejected or do I sit at home and be rejected? There is a funny meme about how single people say there is no one to date or something, and they want to find love, but it's kind of hard to find love when you are at home drinking wine in your pajamas. Me to the T.

I do this with my girlfriend too. She says stop looking, blah blah blah. Ok. So I stop looking, weeks later I'm telling her how lonely I am and she says well let's go out. So I'm out on the town, minding my own business, and not paying attention to any guy…. Pretty sure I'm going home alone, unless I make the first move. Guys are so ridiculous, they're all cowards. Yes ALL. Until proven wrong ;) I've been rejected so many times, that my little heart and ego isn't good at rejection anymore. I used to be fearless and getting shot down was like something I used to purposely go out and do, just so I can narrow the playing field. The last time I got hit on at a bar was March 2018. Picture it, Sicily 1935. From what I can totally recall as a complete, clear as day hit on. I friend requested him the next day and he accepted. And that was the end of our relationship. Like really guy? Sober him was all like naw no thanks, but drunk him was all like oh I want your babies….wth. Now this doesn't count *Drunky Drunkerson* who walked into the Sports Corner when I was working with his own cooler full of alcohol, just walking around town all day. Yeah, sorry buddy. Hard pass. I actually told him I couldn't serve him anymore, because he was 'that guy'.

I would never get a typical movie relationship chase of: girl walks into bar, guy notices girl, girl is too busy to notice guy, guy walks over to girl, girl plays hard to get, guy continues to flirt until guy gets girls number…. It's just not my real life situations. EVER. As Charlotte would say in Sex in the City: "Where is he, I'm 40 years old, I'm exhausted!" Or something of that sort. I felt that deep in my bones when she said that.

#TINDER

By a show of hands, how many of you have heard of Tinder. It gets a bad wrap, because idiots use it. I haven't actually been on any Tinder dates, that I can recall. I've been on two Match dates, which I'll briefly touch on. But Tinder is a free version of Match. It's a free app, where you swipe your finger left or right on people's profiles (pictures) depending on if you are attracted to them or if you like their cheesy bio or big Rock Bass they are holding up. Swiping left means NO, swiping right means, HELLLLLOOO THERE. If they swipe right on you too, you've got a match. So here's the thing. So you get matched up, and nothing happens.

When I first got Tinder, I was all excited, optimistic, and just swiping right on everyone because I didn't want to hurt anyones' feelings, well after two years of an on and off relationship with Tinder, I have grown thick skin. I actually did indeed meet someone like in the first five swipes, we chatted and he was super adorbs and then all of a sudden like three weeks later, he got a girlfriend. Eyeroll: Ok. Deleted the app. I've decided I didn't need a man to define me or to help validate who I am and make me feel worthy. No, I need a man to help me with the chores, tell me I'm pretty, cut my grass, build me things, walk aimlessly in Walmart with and feed me. That's why I need a man. Using Tinder used to be a quick ego boost when you and the dude both swipe right, and then you are like oh hey you have hot buns. Then two days later they reply, "lol thanks." WTF am I supposed to do with "lol thanks". Have some balls and write me back. And two days later? You are fucking lazy. If you have the app, it's basically like being at a blind date convention and you have to be freaking present. Otherwise you are lazy and I am deleting the app again, because you have just reminded me why I deleted it in the first place.

Being over here in Michigan on a peninsula that only goes up for me. I get a lot of Wisconsin tail. You can get a lot of non-promising dudes on Tinder..... 30 miles away.... across the Bay......::eyeroll:: So strap on your ice skates ladies were going on a deadly adventure. Next! I've tried Door County bro's multiple times, we talk for two days, then I'm always like what's the point. I can barely schedule a good time with friends locally, let alone go to Walmart and buy things I don't need, who has time to go on a date, that is probably not going to work, you may get chopped into pieces, he won't want to move to me and I can't move to him. Just dumb.

I used to love, love. Now I am skeptical. I just roll my eyes a lot, swear, and visit my corner gas station for snacks. Gary is actually a really good listener as long as I also buy him a Little Debbie, he bums me a smoke and we chat outside inhaling the freshly pumped gas. So what triggered these comments is I started swiping again, after I went to Tinder rehab and found the deep down secret as to why I feel I need to keep downloading and deleting, and my shrink (who is actually myself) found out, I do it because I get bored and because my hopeless romantic is still trying to sucker punch the cold hearted bitch in the junk and get her outta there. So with swiping this morning, I saw a lot more catfishes than normal, and no, not the fish the guys hold up in the boat. Like who the F cares you caught smallmouth bass on the Mississippi… can you keep my goldfish alive? Should I pick you because you care about my cat, hahah my cat. Also, I am not being racists here, but we live in a 95% white community, and I see an awfully lot of black dudes 1 mile away from me, who I have NEVER seen in my life, so I wonder if those are Tinder bots trying to catfish me into going on a Mexican vacation with them never to be seen again. Probably be mixed up in their ninja for a protein shake. I'm full of protein.

So I'll read you a couple of my Tinder options.

His name is Bo, 31, from Concordia University - Saint Paul, holding a guitar, Asian origin, says I can find him stuffing his face at a local diner on first ave, also says Minneapolis living. So how he is 19 miles away from me, is very questionable. His pictures tell me he travels, like taking artsy photos and is catfishing me, next.

Keith, 34, High Tech High Graduate School of Education (made up I presume) He is a Satellite Technician who can hold a job, is stable, kind and has good manners. He's not wearing a shirt and his second picture is of him fighting in the ring. Now Keith, is fighting really good manners and kind? Next. He's probably not a catfish, but he just didn't send me any vibes.

Brandon, 32, is really into the song 'Sunflower', has a mustache and only takes pictures with his whole head in the frame. Has a Mexi mustache and is trying to see what the *app* is all about. I'll tell you what the app is about Brandon, it's about growing you some tuff skin and saying NEXT. And in order to go to the next picture you HAVE to say yes or no, they don't even give you a 'would rather not say' category. Because I have had a few guys where I wait on them for days, because maybe they're local and I don't want to swipe the wrong way and have them think I want their babies.

Ok last one, Joshua, 31, has one picture of him on a beach, full close cut beard, holding his flip flops, has all his clothes on, 1 mile away, but has one picture, Catfish. Assholes.

#TINDERCONTINUED

When I first joined Tinder I was a hopeless romantic, but after a few days, delete, then reinstall. I'm using it strictly for entertainment purposes now. Sometimes I'll swipe right, just to tell them that they are such a good chef and their pictures are amazing and I wish I could eat their lobster they've prepared. Then I'll unmatch myself. #ghosted.

The latest guy had all these acronyms....like dtf, nsa, brb, asl... lol. Remember Yahoo chat? We were totally meeting our future boyfriends on that thing. That was the original catfish. You broads think you catfish now... pssssh sit down. There was *NO* proof your name wasn't Veronica and didn't wear a size 32 DD, weighed 120 points, were 18 years old and resided on a yacht in Florida. No proof. Nobody ever used their real name; it was 'idle' names. Like Nysnc4Life or Lemons23 or bffandever18. We were so creative, and now, it's like JohnWallace45, Whoopty doo John Wallace, I'm Allyson10. But what is your asl anyways, let's chat. So the one acronym dude, we both swiped right, instant looooovvvvve connection. But he just wanted my goodies and I just wanted to know what nsa stood for. It was not a match made in heaven because we had different agendas. But it was an honest pure love, with no judgements, and come to find out nsa stands for No Strings Attached. Duh. We honestly wished each other well, and I unmatched us. Tear. It was like a super respectable, best seven minute relationship I've ever had. Like we covered the basics. He was like hey let's do it, I was like no. I was like what does nsa stand for, he said no strings attached, and if I ever want to hook up I'll call him. Gosh I miss him. What's his name again?

Then last night, I found a guy, with just jeans on, suspenders, a beard, fire red hair, and straddling a chainsaw. I mean, how could I not? I sent the pics to my girlfriends and they gave me the go ahead. As bad as I wanted to swipe right, I went left. I didn't even know where to start with that profile. I once met a guy who was like my 2nd Tinder boyfriend. We talked for like 3 months. He didn't eat meat, first red flag, but I was ok with that, he ate a lot of cheese and I love cheese, no problem. Then I find out he doesn't drink beer, well.. I mean….. That's ok sweetie as long as I can drink profusely until you are a little cuter. The last red flag where I was mind boggled was he was an Atheist. Three months of my time, only to find out he was a devil worshiper. He was cute, so Jesus took the wheel. So now, in my profile I strictly say "Must love God, meat and beer." I kid you not. Aint nobody got time to waste three months on someone who doesn't drink beer. COME ON!

#HINGE

So, there are some songs or memes, I don't know, but they're about the dating app *Hinge*. Like all the coolest shit in online dating. Where you answer questions, people like your comment or comment back on a photo, then you can decide if you want to match or not. So I comment on some dudes stuff, and crickets, no love connection. And all the guys that do comment on my shit are like way scary. Hinge is worse than Tinder, I honestly fear for my life on Hinge. Tinder is like safe. Tinder, hire a girl.

Speaking of Hinge, I did eventually get a match. So his question that he answered on his profile was 'ideal first date' And he said "late season Sunday Packer Game." And he is cute, so I commented: "Incorrect: Noon Brewer Game. " Because this girl gots swagger. So then he 'invited' me to start the chat. Like wtf does that mean? He can't start the conversation himself? Why do I have to come up with something witty to say first? My profile is already the bee's knees, why would I have to start the conversation…. Later to find out, because he's' only 22. Homeboy is still living at mom's house. Seriously Hinge, I put my acceptable men ages at like 31-46, and I get 22. I guess I'm just too cool and good to be matched with people who have any kind of intellect, maybe own their own house, have a working car. No Hinge just screws me and gives me a selection of early 20 year olds who still live at home and stick out their tongue in pictures because it's the new duck face. Error Hinge, you suck. Useless. I want old school shit. Like a mutual friend. How do I get to the point in my life, where I delete apps, and don't reload them and I just kinda do me? Just do me. Hahah. Damn I'm sexy. Insert:: Duck face selfie::

#HINGECONTINUED

It's all very depressing. Like, I'm on there for love, and most dudes are just DTF, and actually say that in the profile like that's not a sleazy thing to say. But there are some funny dudes on there. For example: "I'm looking for a crazy girl who cries everyday, over reacts and loves me". No lie, that was someone's profile. So naturally I slowly raise my hand. Help, my name is Allyson and I am all those things. But I'm so old. I'm like Charlotte, in Charlotte's Web: Super wise, slow moving, laid a couple eggs, next my death.

#MATCH

You would think that there would be some solid peeps on there, since it's a paid subscription. Like $20 or $30 a month? I'll have to dig deep into one of my blogs and take material from there, because all I can remember from Match is Vanilla Ice and Lord Farquaad. I know, two shady ass characters, one who ends up in rehab and one who gets eaten by a dragon. Metaphors anyone? I dated them both, for a hot second.

Vanilla, I was like nope, the second he showed up at my house, and thought of every excuse why I couldn't' see a movie with him and Lord Fawquad actually had talk of another date, but I just couldn't find time, and maybe subconsciously didn't want to make time? We were going to go fishing and I didn't really want to spend $30 on a license for a *maybe*.

Single Men Take Notes: When you go on a date, wear clothes to match the date! If you don't think you need styling help, you are indeed incorrect. Call your mother, call your friend's mother, go to TJMaxx and ask a sales rep to help you pick out an adult outfit. I am trying really hard not to hurt feelings here.

I'll take you on both of my dates… you are super fucking welcome. Take a seat people, buckles optional.

Date 1: Lord Farquaad (Pre-judgements on him: he was a boring texter, but super cute in his pictures, so of course I want to meet in person) Scene intro and expectations: Red Arrow Park – walking on the ice shoves, maybe grab a beer after. (perfect right?) I pull up, Lord Farquaad drives a nice truck, he is cute, dressed decently. Me thinking: high pitched voice squinting eye:: He is wearing like a waffle knit top that says Old Navy on it, his pants were good and his shoes. I'm wearing a long sleeve grey top with a navy blue winter vest, jeans and sneaker/flat shoes. So our outfits match. He was very quiet, shy-ish, we did talk, he helped me up a couple questionable falls to my death on these ice mountains. We walk back to the cars and I ask him if he wants to go grab a beer, because I'm ok continuing the date. "I don't drink beer" he explained about headaches...yada yada, he's a cheap date… yada yada, but we ended up at Iron Works. He paid for my drink, good job buddy. We have a couple weird pauses and he smiles at me a few times like wtf do I say next… and I said "Welp, I'm good" So we hugged goodbye. I told him thanks for the date, like the damn lady I am. He asked for a 2nd and I said yes hesitantly in my head and I haven't talked to him since. So I think things are going really well.

Date 2: Vanilla: Pre-judgements on him: His texts were awesome! Used a lot of exclamations, kept my interest, felt like I could say anything and he'd roll with it, his pictures resembled Vanilla Ice – so of course I was leary but of COURSE had to meet him in person… and he said "what time should I pick you up"? Good job Vanilla.

Scene intro and expectations: Casual dinner and Super Troopers II. So I knew he was down to clown and was chill, just like me – A1A Beach1 Avenue. He pulls up, in a beater red car…. oh crap - ok breath Allyson, it's ok… he gets out, comes to the door, I open my door and am like Hi! He opens the car door for me, good work son. He's ok looking, maybe his personality will help… Can I tell you what just really pissed me off from ten seconds in? I'm wearing these painted on jeans, bootie heels, a sexy top with holes cut out for the shoulder with a mesh chest area (kinda) and a brown leather jacket. He is wearing white high top sneakers, casual jeans and a plain navy blue sweatshirt and a Tigers Hat. He's a bit rougher than I expected… By the time we got to the SubShop, I thought about having a family emergency, but somehow pushed through and made it through the night. He paid for everything. Good job Vanilla. (eventually the bitch needs to pay for something, maybe date three) He did follow up the next day with a hello and I just plain out said I wasn't as interested as I originally was.

#CATFISH - FOUR OFFENSES

The true definition of a catfish from yahoo is:

Cat·fish /ˈkatˌfiSH/

noun

- **1.** a freshwater or marine fish with barbels resembling whiskers around the mouth, typically bottom-dwelling.
- **2.** another term for wolffish

verb

- **1. f**fish for catfish: "we catfished until the wee hours"

- **2.** lure (someone) into a relationship by means of a fictional online persona:

Since having a presence in the online dating world, I've become super savvy. I'm not bragging, trust me. I've had four catfish in about two months. You could say I'm quite the fisherman.

Nobody cut me up into little pieces, so here are my journeys to love :: raspy Metallica voice:: Turn the paaaggeee.

#INSTA-FISH #FIRSTSTOFFENSE

Sigh. His name is Bryan Wills. I will be using their so-called names because I want America to go find them and punch them in the junk. At the end of our relationship I was keeping Bryan around simply for the enjoyment of fucking around. Like messing with 'its' head. Like oooh baby I miss talking to you, I think about you all the time. But at first I was like hmmm, ok, seems legit, then I started asking military people I knew, if they were able to do certain tasks, such as video chat and take photos, and they all said yes. Then I asked a couple people to creep his insta- one said yes he was real and one was suspicious. Like he's super cute, I hoped he was real, then again, if he's real and he's talking to me in week three how he wants to put a ring on it. Bitches bow down. Which tells me he's probably a psychopath. I know all the red flags for those people.

The first one is moving way too fast. Mushy gushy, lovey dovey..... I've been screwed so many times with guys just not following through or losing interest I basically talked myself out of him. Which is prob good, because I would have ended up on a milk carton. So I'm playing along with Bryan and he really knows not much about me, but has laid it on thick. Thicker than an eyebrow of an 18 year old. What can I say about this Mr. Wills? He's a soldier fighting in Afghanistan, can't call me or video chat me because he's in high security. So currently, we are talking about who would move to live where.

"Baby, would you want to move here?" he asks.

"Oh yeah in 15 years."

(Like he knows I have kids)

"What's it like in MI?"

I explained a little bit of our summers and treacherous winters/fall/spring/summer

"That sounds nice, he said."

He said it sounded nice and the next thing I said was *"Yes you should totally move here."*

Now, that is me playing with the catfish's whiskers. In any normal conversation saying that within 2-3 weeks is wrong....... so I mean, I know he's in fake Afghanistan but come on! He's probably in his mom's basement. He had me go on Google hangout for some reason and it's weird, and it tells you when he's been active. It will show times when he messages me, knowing that sometimes it was 3:30 a.m. and sometimes 4:00 p.m. and no consistent times, just don't add up..... Then my boyfriend bot asked how expensive houses were here, how the schools were.... he's in Afghanistan, his wife died, his mom lives with his sister in Italy, his dad also passed, he can't video chat with me, it's the classic tail of a man who cried wolf.

So I backed off a little more than usual, he told me he was going on a secret mission and would be so dangerous and to be safe and he misses me....... two days later he's back (on the day he also said he was supposed to be moving back in Florida), sent me some crap on how scary the journey was ——— and then surprise surprise..... left Instagram? Like deleted his profile. His comment on one of my photos is still there.... but he either blocked me or died. Pretty sure he just died and the government erased his identity and made his existence, non. Because baby, we were getting married.......

That was my first, but not last catfish experience. We have three more to go.

#INSTA-FISH #SECONDOFFENSE

Man I'm a fucking keeper. Rack em up.

His name is Anthony Mask. He is from California and lives in Long Beach. How did I really know he was living in his mom's basement? Because his abs were an 8 pack. Nobody EVER with an 8 pack has ever even looked at me. He is also overseas fighting for his country. Oh how very fucking noble. Every single catfish is giving the military a bad wrap. Also the Navy, but maybe my buddy Jake is in my next book. I asked Anthony why he liked me and this was his response.

"Cos of your great sense of humor and I would like to spend my life with you," he said.

His dad left him and his mom, so his mom raised him and his mom is now dead. He sold his house, his phone was also broken by a 'pirate' a few days before so he has to use the military computer. So this morning, I'm like damn, I'm wasting a lot of time on these douchebags. So I told Anthony that I was no longer going to speak to him while he was away and he never responded. And I blocked him on instagram. Two more.

#HINGE-FISH #THIRDOFFENSE

By now, I'm fed up. I'm pissed that these little weiners are sitting in their basement with crazy eyes trying to get in my sexy pants. Hinge-fish: Yes, hinge. His name was Robert Gomez, and the fact that he was a man of color totally made me think that he was real. He got me by saying "hey beautiful" That was all it took and I was like "Sir, yes sir." I don't usually go for the light brown chocolate, but shit he was really cute and had nice sized arms. His profile was about people being real and honest and heartbreak. So I immediately was like, me too! And we clicked on that. Then he said something that threw me off. I told my girlfriend about our early pre-nup and about 3 minutes later...

"He's not on facebook" she said.

"Red flag #1, I replied.

So I said to Gomex. "Are you on Facebook?"

He said no because people are always trying to screw with people on social media.... Lol ok pal.

"Well do you have Instagram or Snap Chat because I need proof that you are real."

And guess what little Robert did? .... He surprisingly vanished. Apparently he didn't want to spend the rest of his days with me. Onto my final catfish.

#HINGE-FISH #FOURTHOFFENSE

By now, I'm just being a bitch to these fellas looking for love. He matched me, regular looking American. White, bald, bigger build. Minus the bald, white and bigger it's actually how I like them. Not fat, but meaty. Like a meatball. Just like me! We would have made the most perfect meatball sandwich. But guess what. After telling him I wanted to pinch his butt (not really) I asked him if he had Facebook or Instagram. He said no. So I simply replied, then you are a catfish and goodbye. And guess what happened. He deleted me.

Did I learn my lesson? Was there even a lesson? The first couple are like wait, are they, no they're not. Everyone has good hearts and nobody is creepily in their basements eating cheetos and drinking beer at this time of day. Sure shit they are. And now, all my friends, I will never get back those five solid weeks that I was romanced by two different Afghani's and two Hingers, only to be left in a pile of my own shit. Well played losers, well played.

REASONS WHY I WILL NOT DATE YOU OR JUST STOP TALKING

1. You are overseas on tour.
2. You don't drink beer.
3. You don't eat meat.
4. Both of your parents have passed, or one died and the other doesn't live anywhere near you. It must be because you are a psychopath.
5. You are too sweet too soon.
6. Your English sucks.
7. I will run real fast if you are in the military.
8. You don't eat cheese.
9. Your dog is in your dating profile more than 1 photo. You are lame. It's a dog.

#NOTTODAYCRAIG

I'm tired of having to think like a guy. How about those bastards feel like what it's like to be a woman? Hormones up and down, holding the world up with a finger most days. How about no, Craig. *YOU* don't piss me off. Think before you talk and put my panties on and see what it feels like to have 1,000 hormones gushing through my heart at one time. Not today Craig, not today.

RANDOM DATING THOUGHTS

1. Figuring out the 'wait time' for texting is exhausting.
2. Getting 20 year olds in the swipe column and figuring out their stupid acronyms of letters
3. Online dating is like sitting on a cactus without underwear
4. Being single is like losing your ice cream cone with one lick to the ground
5. Being single is like getting into the shower in the gym, realizing you forgot your shampoo in your bag
6. Dating sucks

#IWILLDIESINGLE

I 99.9% feel I was meant to be single. I can't even do the first one to two weeks. Who am I kidding, after the first one to two days of not even officially dating, my relationship is over. Ok Fine! I can barely make it through the first one to two hours. Okay actually, the first one to two hours, piece of cake, I don't even like you like that yet. So I'm cool.

Oh you're texting me, great, let me just not pay any attention and do life. Take a long shower, cut the grass, shovel some snow, watch a whole season of Reno 911.

But what? It's hours later and you think I'm cute and you like looking at me? It's over. Compliment me and I'm yours. (One more compliment away from taking a scandalous picture) But still, I'll play the game in my head the best I can. But after I start getting in my own head, I'm toast. I just quit. I either text right away thinking who cares, I'm not playing games, or I check the clock and give myself a waiting period. Both of those options kill me in the end. Dead on arrival.

A. I'm old, so I think why am I playing games. If I see a text pop up, and I'm not busy, I'll read it and give a good response.

B. I'm old, so I also think, ok Al, you could die anyday, play it fucking cool and dangle the bate… do not answer him right away. And now I'm here on hour 12 of a new prospect thinking, sayonara buddy. It's not you, it's me.

For real. I'm not cool. The anxiety of waiting for the next morse code, picture like on Facebook and even worse, snap back of something amusing is just torture. It's not fun. I guess I'll just keep my sex men in my back pocket and hit them up when I need a fix. Because not one relationship I have ever had, started as a hookup. That stuff is in fairytales. Fairytales that I don't star in. I am who I am. I am the most honest person you will ever meet. And I am here to say, I cannot play it cool.

#PEOPLEWHOMEETPEOPLERIGHTAWAY

My next point - how in the world are these people who *JUST* breakup or just got divorced, or hell, not even divorced yet fall in love with someone else. Like where in the hell did they go and meet this person. I don't know how people jump from relationship to relationship. Or marriage to marriage. I mean I guess I know *HOW* they do, but I want to know how they find these people. And where do I find one for me?! Whether these people are actually right for them is up to them, I dunno. They say people settle. Well, I'm sorry, but if I don't mesh with you or you smell funny or you remind me of some other guy I dated, I can't do it. I won't even pretend for the sake of someone to hang out with. There was this guy a couple summers ago, I just couldn't. He was gorgeous, had the same interests as me, but something was just off and I felt weird when I was around him like, just wasn't right. When we broke up, my ex that he actually reminded me of, was like sad about it, told me I should try it again with him (thanks for the relationship advice) and I guess whatever, we were having a heart to heart on relationships for some stupid reason, I actually gave that person another thought in my head and then shook myself out of it. No, there is a reason why people break up. There is a reason why things don't work out. But for real, where do I go to find a rebound and showcase a newfound love? I can't even wrap my head around it. I need a cold shower.

#THEILLUSTRATEDMAN

We first connected eyes at the gym. He had questionable tattoos and tank top choices and his upper body seemed to be more developed than his legs. So I was sadly an inner b*tch and I assumed he skipped leg day, but nonetheless, he still caught my eye. After one year of saying the sheepish hellos, we met by the coffee pot. He smiled with his eyes, soulful, I found out a lot in the five minutes we talked, then the whole one year of meaningless hello's.

Now when I see him weekly, because of that talk, he smiles with all of his teeth, and he has them all ;) And I am hesitant. I clasp my lips together and flash a weird smirk because I can't look at him for longer than five seconds without looking away. I'm just awkward. He seemed smarter than me and seemed much older. I like older guys, they just do it for me. They know what they want and get the job done. Most are confident and they seem to want a woman who can handle their greatness. They don't want a bimbo. My self doubt has gotten the best with this one. Will The Real Slim Shady please stand up? I used to crave rejection, just crossing off the names and moving onto the next like a serial killer.

He finally asked me out. Bold. I was impressed and happy that I waited. I had just finished some shameful deadlifts and was sweating like a mother. He wore the pants and I was impressed, a man, a man who took charge! Little did he know the day before I ate a ½ pan of brownies, but that's off topic.

The feelings were shut down as fast as they were built up. I found out he had a lot of drama. Now I understand that people have skeletons, but some of his skeletons were still scratching at his door. I honestly wondered what my eyes looked like when he was talking. I tried hard not to respond and wait about five seconds to process like a good girlfriend would do. Trying to be supportive and listen, I bit my tongue a lot for that 30 minutes. The longest relationship I've had in awhile.

#STONERS

Why don't you date a stoner.? Because they're stoners. That's all there is to it. Anyone who says 'Oh I smoke pot, and I always will' is usually someone you can say peace out to. Unless you are also a stoner. I don't have a problem with those who do it, but just call me back. I am just going to voice my opinion here and be firm on believing that Stoners have researched hours and hours on topics of marijuana because they just need points to prove to people that it's ok to do daily. If that makes sense. Back in November I went on a few dates with one. Then he dropped off the face of the earth, do you know why? Because he probably just forgot to message me back. Then as he's sitting in a blaze, he thinks about me and laughs and says "oh yeah."

They're so laid back, they put no effort in. This is coming off rude, but it's also rude to *NOT* get a hold of me back. A wholesome young peach from Georgia (false) like myself. Another man, who was really cute, seems nice, came out of his closet within 15 minutes of talking to me, and asked if it was a deal breaker. This usually means in code : I smoke pot, so if I forget to communicate at all with you, it's because I am indeed high." and they think it's a get out of jail free card. So back to the cute guy. We text all day, after hours and hours of back and forth we end the conversation. The next day, I reached out to him regarding our night date turning into a day update, he said "No problem," and that was it. Today, no communciation. So two days ago he liked getting to know me and there were no red flags, and then today, nothing.

Being too busy is such a lie. People make time for who they want to make time for, end of story. Make an effort brofessor, or next.

"I wasn't gonna run from the cops, but I was high."

#DEARLOSERS

If you have ever chased a girl, for a year, finally got her, and then ghosted her, you might be a loser. If you have ever chased a girl for over 3 months, got her, then ghosted her, you are a loser. This girl is me, I'm the girl.

#THANKSFORTHESUGGESTION

A comment was made to me on my dating game by an anonymous donor: And I quote:

"Maybe you would have a boyfriend if you didn't write about them all the time."

I ended that quickly with "Maybe guys shouldn't be idiots."

#FONDULAC

Being freshly single, when myself and two other gals went to a random bar in BFE, we ended up hanging out with some of the locals. We started talking to them belly up before dinner and then after dinner met up for a drink. Dummy me. So one of the guys looks handsdown like Justin Timberlake, only Timberlake is like a ten and this guy is like a 6.9. But nonetheless, three beers he woulda been an 8.2. So I kind of hit on him, more in my head, than actually outloud. But I finally mustered up the courage to tell him that he looked like Timberlake.

He replied "Bye, bye, bye.'

Things didn't work out.

#WHATDOYOUDESERVE

You deserve to be loved. You deserve to be respected and appreciated. If it's early on in the relationship, reach out at least every other day. Honestly for women, we like it if you reach out a couple times a day, but we are actually good once a day. How hard is it to say - hey how's your day going? Or, I'm on my break whatcha up to? Or I just swallowed an eggshell. Like, be available. Don't make us feel like we don't matter. Society tells us these days, that if he's thinking about you, he'll get ahold of you. So, when you don't reach out all day long until 8pm, you didn't think of me until then? I call shenanigans. We want to be on your mind. We want *you* to be the man. We want you to be persistent and take the lead. As women, we are taught to be strong, and independent, but really deep down, we just want to be cared for. We want you to put a blanket on us while we're watching tv, we want you to bring the car in and get an oil change, we also want you to make your own damn doctor appointment.

Like if it seems manly or personal, a man should do it. Then fucking do it. Please. Take the reins on: fixing household things, getting a new latch for the fence, calling the sewer guy, anything car related, killing spiders, make your own doctor appointments, fixing loose screws on anything, figuring out why the wifi stopped working, keeping the fridge stocked with beer, getting gas for anything, cut the grass. Honestly, I would cut the grass fine.

Things I feel like a woman should do: deep clean, laundry, kiss boo-boos, decorate the house, shop for *your* clothes, bake cookies and eat them, pack the suitcases for trips and camping, grocery shop, find a daycare/school for the kids, vacuum, dust. I'll cook as long as you aint fancy.

Life is hard, dating is hard. It's super hard these days because there are so many avenues of dating. So I think it's harder for people to settle down because there are all these options, I mean, not my options, but you know. You's guys, match me up at a barbeque.

#DIVORCE

#MYMOSTBEAUTIFULMISTAKE

I will never forget watching the movie *Eat, Pray, Love*, and bawling my eyes out, feeling better and yet worse, because I was there, I knew exactly what the main character was feeling.

Julia Roberts' character says: "The only thing more unthinkable than leaving was staying; the only thing more impossible than staying was leaving. I didn't want to destroy anything or anybody. I just wanted to slip quietly out the back door, without causing any fuss or consequences, and then not stop running until I reached Greenland." *Eat Pray Love*

Whether you want a divorce or not, it all sucks. It's like jumping out of a plane and realizing half way you don't have a parachute. We are all wired with big hearts, feelings, emotions, logic, fight and drive to succeed, so when something impacts your life so much such as love does, and it fails, it's tragic. I cried for what felt like six weeks straight. Living at my parents house. I would have panic attacks and anxiety when they would have to leave the house even to get groceries. I was not well.

But I wanted this, didn't I? You know? You always wish for a happy life, wonderful 'things' and a great man. I always knew something was off and had to get out.

The marriage made me second guess every single thing I've known about life's beauty and especially what love is supposed to be. I was exhausted and confused but still after all, I was in love and so I fought for us. I stayed for hope. Hoping the good times would last, the fighting would stop and was waiting for the good to outweigh the bad. I made excuses about what kind of love I deserved, excuses about why we were both stressed out and miscommunicated, excuses on what I thought love was supposed to be. In the end, I compromised 90% of the relationship just to keep someone happy who would never truly be happy. That's as far as I will go down that road.

Maybe I'm pathetic, but sometimes when I look at him now and our eyes really connect, I truly believe that somewhere deep down, he truly loved me with all he could and to this day still wants to give me the things I need, but he can't. So he continues to run to where it's easy and safe. A place he doesn't have to deal or fix anything. He was my high school love, the one I broke up with to go to College, my first everything so I feel there is always something special about that and it connects you more to them than anyone else. Three or four years after I finished college, we reconnected at Dino's Bar and that was it. The force field was unstoppable.

I'm in a different kind of love for him now. I love him for the man I wish he was, the man I see when his intentions are pure and the way our kids love him. But after all is said and done, I still can't change anything, except my own direction.

#MOTHERHOOD

#COOLMOM

I'm not like most moms, I'm a cool mom. Just kidding. I am not, at all. I use my mom tone in public, I use my mom tone when my kids friends are over, and I give '*gonna lose my shit warnings*' but only at home, when mom is '*this close*' to losing it. I have recently told my children that I am allowed one swear word a day. I didn't use one today, so that means I get two tomorrow.

My daughter loves me and being at my house and my son loves dad and being at his house. I mean, they probably drink beer in their underwear, eat beef sticks and cheese, watch sports and play minecraft all day. I mean, sounds pretty good. I don't know why my daughter likes my house, but I hope it never fades. I'm sure she'll go through a phase of hating me, as all daughters do. But, I'm pretty average. I think as moms we all slack at some parts of our duties. Like me, for instance, HATE cleaning. Like hate. Honestly, until recently, I passed it off as being lazy, but now that I think about it, it's because I flippin hate it. I'd rather go to the dentist and get a tooth pulled than mop something. So I decided to get a cleaning lady. And I personally know this cleaning lady so I trust her not to judge me because God knows she knows way more 'dirt' (insert forced laugh::

hrhhrhhrhrhhrr) than what's in my house. It's not the clutter part or organizing, it's deeper. The bathrooms, kitchen floor and piles of dust, and cobwebs. Yes, sounds super disgusting. Well yeah. I knew I needed a cleaning lady when the past two weeks, I'd go to the bathroom, and look behind the door and against the walls and see dirt specks, hair balls and misc fluff. And you know what I did about it? Nothing. My brain is so packed full of other useless garbage, that by the time I wiped and flushed, that dirt was long gone from my to do list. Hell, when I realize I need more eggs and need to add eggs to my grocery list, by the time I grab a pen the thought is out of my mind and I'm on the computer checking my online banking situation, which then takes me to facebook, back to the bank, to paypal to see if the payment cleared, to facebook, hotmail, to the bank. You get it. So then those 3 or 4 times I go to the bathroom that day at home, the same thing comes to mind.

So I'm just going to do it. I grew up with a cleaning lady with my parents, so let's keep it going. It's not that I don't have time, because I do - ish. It's that I don't wanna. I mean, you know. It's hard enough for me to get my duffle bag, purse and random items on my passenger seat inside, then have to yell at my kids who are already racing into the house to come back and take their backpacks, crusty crumbs and water bottles, etc. So when I get in the house, the kids kick their shoes off, throw down their bags, and I'm in my own hell trying to even fit in the door with my accumulated crap from the day, cursing the whole time I am cleaning out my bags.

The kids are kind of trained, they're pretty good. I let them get away with things, but not everything, especially if it's easy things, like putting your shoes not in front of the door. Ok, so I do say weekly to the kids, I need your help. I need you to put your jacket away, I need you to clean your clothes off the bathroom floor. I need you to throw away your band aid wrapper, throw away the used smoke bombs on your floor from Fourth of July, the floor is not a garbage can… you get it. A lot of times daily, I try to give them the poor me, but not as dramatic, and I say "Do you see anyone else around here besides me, you and your brother/sister (depending who's in my firing range)? Ok, well I need your help" weekly.

One day, when they are my age and have two to three kids and I'm on an island in Tahiti, they're gonna say sorry Mom for throwing my shit all over the house and sucking. And here is my apology to my mom, "Mom, I'm sorry for sucking. You are the best." To this day If I brought my laundry over to my mom and dad's house, I can almost guarantee she would still do it for me. #loveyou

#TUBBYTIMETHOUGHTS

It was tubby time, which sometimes I cringe, but the outcome of your kids looking like Gap models is just amazing. It's awesome what a little soap and water will do to turn those Gremlins into Kardashians.

#KIDSARECRAZY

I don't know about you, but kids are a handful. I know, it's the circle of life, it's what mama bears do, we reproduce. I don't know if it's because I'm a Hot Mess Mom that I struggle, but most days I'm just happy to keep the kids alive. I say that just as a statement, because thinking about it, I have really wonderful kids for the most part, but they urk me. They won't starve to death because they can get their own snacks and for the most part get their own beverages. They won't die in some unsafe environment…. Well maybe, my daughter does so many handstands against random objects, lately she's been using the window and door, so just waiting for a foot through glass there.

As I was folding laundry the other day I had each kids pile nicely stacked and thought I'd try something new. Like asking for help putting clothes away. Madi, please take these pants and tops and put them in their right drawers. So she takes the pile, makes a pit stop at the bathroom, sets them on the bathroom counter, goes to the bathroom, comes back to the living room, does a handstand.

"Madi, your clothes, " I said.

"'Ohhh I was just doing that."

So phew, clothes away. Turns out, I go into her room about an hour later, her clean clothes are shoveled in a pile, like a tossed salad, against the wall against the dresser. Blank stair. She literally had two more feet to them away and chose to grenade bomb them against the wall.

And my son is just difficult. His favorite word is No. I think he was worse than my daughter at his age. His first response to anything I say is 'No'. In my nicest mommy voice ever "Colt, here are your clothes, please get dressed." And mind you, he is laying on the chair watching Paw Patrol with his hands down his pants like Al Bundy. Ok, no he isn't.

When asked to get dressed he says "No."

"Colt please just get dressed so you can keep watching Paw Patrol."

He grunts back. Four minutes later, he's in the same spot. Mommy voice gets a little more annoyed.

I press pause on the remote and say "Colt get dressed now"

"Noo….. ugh fine" He grumbles.

So each morning it's almost the same. So some people like their kids to match and brush their hair everyday. I really like when my kids can get themselves dressed. Even if it's one of those mornings where it's like oh shit it's 7:15 and we didn't eat yet.

"Kids go get dressed" I say.

 "What should we wear?" they say

"I don't care, just try to match."

Colt comes out in the same clothes he slept in and Madi usually does an ok job.

So anyway, some mornings are a super struggle, because I could have a meeting across town, the bus isn't available for Colt and he was just not into doing anything. So after all day, I get home at 8 pm, haven't been home since 7:35 am and look at the living room floor to a clean pair of black pants. He never changed out of the pants he wore ALL day yesterday and slept in last night. SMH. Perfectly clean, yummy smelling pants. Nope. No wonder why Nana checked him up and down as he went into their house this morning.

#MARYPOPPINS

I swear my mom is Mary Frickin Poppins. When my kids go there, somehow they end up in matching clothes, (she claims they get into water outside??) My daughter's hair is always braided and my son has clean clothes on and they're always in the kitchen baking something with a smile. Whenever I open the door to nana and papa's house when I pick them up, little white doves fly out of the door and my kids teeth sparkle like a cheesy toothpaste commercial. For real. I'm Pippy Longstocking over here and can't afford a shower or a washing machine. So, that's why I say I'm just happy my kids are alive. Mainly because sometimes I want to leave them at home for more than 20 minutes and see how they'll manage. I didn't even raise my voice that high this morning. Progress, not perfection people. I feel like I get comments from her like "well can't you get groceries or run errands with the kids. Or, why don't we organize their clothes this weekend." Which is usually ok, but most of the time, I'm still putting away laundry from three days prior and their backpacks always need emptying, they're shit is just everywhere when we come home. Not to mention, we switch from dads to mine every two days, so three times a fucking week I get a whole bag of goodies to pack, and then drop off and then pick up and then put away. Then two days later, I get to do it again. It's gotta change. I don't even know what day it is most of the time. So to ask me if I can run errands or even do anything with them that revolves around getting things done outside of the house, is ridiculous most school nights.

#DAILYLIVING

I honestly try not to leave the house after 6:30 pm on school nights. At about 7 pm is when they turn into little gremlins and all of a sudden they're voices turn whiney and their legs don't work.

4:30 pm is our average dinner time and the kitchen is cleaned up by 5:30. At that time I'm still putting things away around the house from the morning of us getting ready for the day. All of a sudden it's 6:15 and at 7:00 we do jammies and tv together. And 7:30 is usually us getting ready for bedtime. Lights out 8:30 latest. My bedtime shit is on fleek, but I didn't say my shit was shiny. Owning your own pair of kids is something crazy. Everyday it's like living in the documentary "Naked and Afraid" where you are naked and afraid living in extreme heat with scorpions, bugs, snakes, lions and tigers. Sometimes you get out alive, sometimes you tap out. Most of the time, just as you are about to tap out, aka lose your shit, they do something cute and life is good again. It's like, just when you think you are going to die, you find a really large leaf on a tree to tie on your privates with some shedded snake skin from the Aboriginie jungle.

Chandler Bing:: *I mean could the comparison beeee any better?*

#MYMOM

I remember saying 'ugh there's nothing to eat' when she just went grocery shopping. You know why? Because she didn't buy the garbage that I wanted. I wanted Cheetos and Little Debbies, and all she ever got was freaking nutri grain bars or granola bars….. Welp, history repeats itself. Because, whenever I have the house stacked with deliciously horrible food, guess who actually ends up eating it? Me! They're all nestled in their beds sleeping and I'm nestled in the kitchen with my face over a box of cheese nips and fruit snacks. Fruit snacks are so good once you eat that first bag. I usually take two bags, and throw them in my pocket and walk around the house having little snack times from room to room. Then sit down with cheez-its and side of ranch..... Dip the cheez-its in the ranch. But oh no, my bowl is empty, I think I'll take some pretzels, because I ate all the pringles before the cheez-its and I still have ranch left. It's horrible. Just horrible. It doesn't even taste good. So, if you are reading this and think oh I'll never turn out like my mom. You probably already have, but you just haven't realized it. Mom jeans happen when your muffin top is overflowing, you tuck that shit in and the mom haircut, I feel like that is obsolete, thank God. But yeah, you'll be walking with Bonnie in no time.

#DISLIKES

Things I don't like doing as a mother: waking up to a child yelling my name from the other room, sweeping, mopping, polishing, putting air in my car tire, cleaning toilets or bathrooms, doing laundry (esp putting away) cooking, ugh getting the leafs out of my garage, taking out the garbage, snow blowing, cleaning cobwebs. Basically if you have to put the word cleaning in front of anything or use it in a sentence, you can find me hiding under the bed, where I will find about five hair ties, candy wrappers from Christmas, bobbi pins and dust bunnies.

#LIKES

Things I like doing as a mom: snuggling, watching movies, baking from a box, cutting the grass, organizing and purging, picking my daughter and her friends from school, budgeting, kissing my sons chubby cheeks, going to the library or park, paying bills, driving a minivan, watching sporting events, and stuffing my envelopes, Dave Ramsey style.

#IAMAMEATBALL

I actually like to blame my kids for me being the meatball that I am. When I don't have them due to split parenting time, I can relax, actually look in the fridge for longer than 10 seconds, ponder life a little, track my food, prepare my food, and eat my food, all without someone yelling *MOOOOMMMM* three to four times from either outside or the other room. When they're here, seriously, they run circles around me. Maybe that's why I'm kind of slow moving, because they're so freaking fast like squirrels that in order to keep the earth spinning on it's correct axis, I have to slow down. You are welcome to everyone for keeping everything aligned in the Universe.

When I sit at home, childless, I feel like I'm in the African Forest, crickets chirping, birds flying, lions napping all around me. Pure bliss. When they're here, it's nuts. The other day, my daughter was sitting next to me on the patio bench, I was minding my own business, I think maybe I was writing and she started to breath deep on my arm/shoulder area. On purpose. Like when you breath on a window to make the fog. About 10 seconds in,

"Umm Mads, please stop." She did not. "Mads please stop."

She stopped for a millisecond and continued, so kind of shocked, I swatted at her head and accidently got her eyeball. She starts crying, and I'm like woman! I told you to stop breathing on me.

"Yeah but you pushed my eye."

"Madi I am sorry, but when someone says to stop, please stop, it was annoying me." I said

"Yeah but you didn't have to hurt my eye."

That is the kind of annoyance I get from them. Sure, they love me, it's true, because at any given night, one of them has weaseled their way into my bed and I was just too tired to argue with them to go back to their bed. Those little gremlins, while cute, I just can't sleep with someone else in the bed. So when they're here, there is way less concentration on my part. And damn it Susan, don't even tell me to meal prep or know on Sunday what I'm going to cook the whole week. I can barely get dressed in the morning, let alone remember to pack a towel for my gym bag.

#ENVELOPESYSTEM

When you are on a budget smaller than Guam, you have to budget wisely. So I started doing Dave Ramsey's Envelope system a few years ago to see if I could truly survive on my own. I read the book a long time ago and really only do the envelopes, the $1,000 emergency fund, and the snowball debt. There are many steps to his madness, but I only do the first three steps of however many he has. I wish, oh how I wish I could save for college for my kids, but honestly, I can't. It would be like $10 a month not 10% like he suggests.

There's another step like 'give, pay off your mortgage (eyeroll), invest, and with the first three I'm like meh I'm good. It gives me anxiety waiting those three to five days before payday. Like, I go to the store and use change. Not because I don't have the money, but because that money is accounted for somewhere else. Like, I'm saving up to remodel my kitchen, it will more than likely take me three years to do that. By using tax money. Which is what I really use for all of my larger purchases for the house. To get it to my liking. We have a huge swing set that is cemented in so it's more than likely, I won't be moving within the next ten years. Maybe not ever. And by the way my love life is going, I'll probably die here.

#BETTYCRACKER

I was not given the gift of cooking. Or the gift of enjoying cooking. I second guess myself on everything, I go to the store to seriously make three new recipes that I don't always make, and I come home with canned soup and pizza crust for diy pizzas and then soup and garlic bread. I'm not cut out for that shit and I'm standing up to myself now saying that it's ok. I am on pinterest, insta and all these gals can whip up a creme brulee in 2 seconds, and I'm like, I'm good at toast. And I'm also really good at making boxed brownies and adding frosting, then those microwaveable pastry treats in a mug. I know you can pinterest dessert in a cup, but I actually just get the mix that is already prepared and all I do is empty the bag and put three tablespoons of water and heat for 1 minute. I mean, genius. So I just got back from the grocery store, and am super hungry, that I'll break down what my mind had the capacity to make.

With all of this information out in the world---- I am making scrambled eggs. Do you know why? Because I know that I can ace scrambled eggs. But here is the ticker, here is the real amazing part, I'm adding in things to it. Like 1/2 block of cream cheese, green peppers, green onions and red onions, because I firmly believe all onions are created equal. Actually, no, white onions but I still eat them just as happily. And then I peaked in my fridge, and to what amazement do I see? I see some corn on the cob that needs to get eaten, so I shuck the kernels off with a knife and toss those bad boys into my vegetable medley mix. So boom. More than likely, I will have to choke it down. But that's how I do it. As I sit down and remembered I was also baking a yukon yellow potato, so I add that to my meal, almost added it to the eggs, but that would have taken longer, so potato, added greek yogurt, gobs of ketchup (whatever, I love ketchup) and my egg concoction. YOLO.

So I think the reason why I don't like to cook is that it's hard, you need to concentrate, you have to add numbers for calorie counting, and there's always more than five ingredients. Well I'd rather cook than clean. Update: I've now added my potato to my eggs, it now looks like trough food on a dairy farm. and I'll eat it. Because damn it, I cooked it.

Update: I left about 1/3 of the food to the garbage, it tasted like garbage and I suck at cooking.

#SORRYIMNOTSORRY

Honestly, thinking about what to cook for my kids sometimes gives me anxiety, and when I was married I had way more anxiety of what my husband would want to eat. So it's halved, and usually it's me cooking what I know they will eat. Like sandwiches, we do a lot of those, things in cans, things in boxes. The last noodle salad I made was out of a box. Sorry Gretchen, those chives aren't freshly diced and that pepper and garlic, not chiseled from my chive board. And that crab salad Karen that I bought at the deli and slapped in my own glass bowl, yup store bought, so no I don't know what kind of fucking mayonaise I used or how much peprika to use. Eat a weiner. So those are my thoughts on cooking.

#WHYILOVEMYDAUGHTER

This is my daughter's writing on our Chromebook, I had to put it in here, so someday when she is old enough to see how cool her mom actually was, she will be so happy to see this.

8 years old: I edited nothing.

I love my mom because...1. she likes gymnastics and softball.

2. She loves me a lot more than 1000000000$ i hope.

3.she feeds me when i want food.

4.i love her too.

5.we have a cool swing set.

6.we also have a cool deck.

7.when i fall down she helps me back up.

8.she encouereges me.

9.she just bought me snacks.

10.and she reads to me.

I love you...

Ps i just wish we did not have colt emma and alec that much you would say NO though.

#BEEPBEEP

There comes a time in every parents life when they question "Should I get a minivan." And usually the answer is no, but somehow mom gets dad to buy one and oh my gosh, stow and go has changed my life. So, after purchasing a family automobile, which I haven't had a car payment in years, I was like ok, where in the fack am I going to come up with an extra $250/month. Dig deep Al, dig deep. Stripper! Yes, I'll strip once a month because now I was a soccer mom with loads of kids coming out of my van, like the car trunk of a Coolio video. Only my kids had mismatched clothes on and chocolate ice cream on their face. I needed to not let it get repoed.

Trying to figure out how to make extra money and actually not strip started to become an issue. But thinking if I strip one time, every two months I should make bank and pay a good chunk down? It would be good right? Just kidding, nobody would pay to see my white girl cheeks. I bet I was a stripper in my last life. Regina got a big ole butt.

So I started bartending. The patrons get whatever drink they can tell me how to make or beer. I'm really good at serving beer. My family gets tappers only, no mixed drinks, I probably pour too much alcohol in the cup to make up for my poor bartending skills and the beer has head. I guess I'd rather give a stiff one..... just like my sex life. Ba-da-ching. There are eight T.V's in the room the size of my kitchen and living room combined, with three remotes. I'm no mathematician, but that doesn't add up. My first four shifts, I waited two hours each time until someone came in to turn the T.V.'s on for me. Thank God, someone to relieve me from my dark thoughts. Someone ordered a screwdriver once, and I had to think hard.

"Ok, so OJ and Vodka?" I said to a handsome younger gentleman.

Thank God he just replied "yes."

I lost some dignity that day but he didn't roll his eyes, so there's that. Update: I have retired from bartending. I enjoy my weekends off, going to Menards, watching the trees in my backyard, you know, the finer things. Tax season will have to help me pay that bad boy.

#GRAMMAJOHNSON

I try to see my gramma as much as I can these days. Whether it's bumming around the Pine Tree Mall, or I bring over some mending, we chat live once in a while. She is the coolest.

As Grandma GG was getting out of our van the other day, my four year old said 'she's going to die soon' as she closed the door. Thank goodness she didn't hear that. He has said it a couple other times to me and I just nod and say yes, she is getting old, so that's why we need to visit her, be extra nice and hang out with her as much as we can.

"Will she go to heaben?"

"Yes she will," I said.

I cringe at the thought of ever losing my grandma. She is honestly like one of my best gal pals. I remember having tons of sleepovers at her house, learning how to crochet and watching 'The Golden Girls' in her and grandpa's room. I always took a bath in her old school tub with the feet on it and she would always powder me up with Talc infested powder that smelled like Wildflowers. I found that same-ish powder on amazon, bought her a container and myself, so that I can hopefully pass those memories to my kids. I don't think my oldest likes the powder, it's weird to her, but my youngest, loves being pampered with it and I love covering his (seriously stinky teenager) armpits, bum bum, feet, neck, etc. and watching him smile at every pat. Every morning waking up at grams, I'd have toast and dip it in some coffee, get on my church clothes and lay in her lap during the sermon as they turned down the lights.

#GRAMMABICKEL

The Bickel side of the family is a little different than the Johnson's, but still as amazing.

When all the aunts, uncles and cousins are in town, we meet at Gramma Bickels, the snacks come out on her kitchen island along with the whiskey, and we sit and rotate who gets to be the captain in front of the on-going 1,000 piece puzzle that is being worked on that week. It's a nostalgic feeling that happens a few times a year and I love it. Gramma and Grampa used to live on the River, right on Kaltenbach, and their house had a particular smell, the garage door always stuck and slammed, but was light in weight. Sometimes you take a left and go upstairs right away, and sometimes you went straight down the stairs, past the pool table to the second 'secret' entrance. Now, the new house, doesn't have as many good memories, but still has the smell.

So as I am aging, I just realize that life is so precious. People will eventually go to 'heaben' and we won't get to keep making the memories we are making now. When your family wants to hang out with you, you do it. When your friends want to hang out with you, you try to do it. When your cousins are in town from Arizona, you visit them, you hug them as weird as it sometimes seems. The Bickel side hugs, and the Johnson's say hi.

#GROWINGUP

I actually don't mind aging. When I was younger, it was like yeah, I'm 13, yeah I'm 18 an adult, then you are like oh crap I'm almost 25, have nothing to show for it, then meet your husband at Dino's, get hitched and you turn 29 thinking when you hit 30, you'll be dead. But, as I get older, there's a sense of relief. A sigh, a cool breeze blowing as you sit on your front porch swing. Each year is a year away from constant self approval. You care less about what people think, you care less about getting six pack abs, and you start becoming way more realistic with life. By the time you are 36, maybe you've been married, have some kids, maybe you're divorced or widowed, but you've learned lessons. You sorta have a grasp on life. Sorta. Until you are on the side of the road because you were determined to wait until tomorrow's payday to get gas, because dammit you're on a budget.

Wherever you are in life, embrace it.

When you are little your parents say "kid, you don't know nothing 'bout nothing, I used to have to walk to and from school, uphill, both ways."

As you age, you realize your parents did know a lot and how they're in their 60's now and have a great core group of friends, go on a lot of vacations, they golf everyday, I mean, how can you not think they know all the secrets of life? So to my parents, who show me daily the finer things in life, and continue to support me, and my life. Not always agree with my decisions, but just knowing that no matter what I do, or where I go, they have my back. So I'm not sad to age, I'm excited. My 30's have been rocky, but I'm alive, and somewhat optimistic where I'm going. When I turn 40, I'm having the biggest bash ever, and you're all invite.

#<u>INMYFEELINGS</u>

#FEBRUARY

Being depressed is a special kind of hell. But being depressed in Winter is even worse. At least in the summer when you are just depressed you can grab a beer and go sit on your patio, close your eyes and take in the sun. And usually talk yourself out of jumping off the Interstate Bridge. But being depressed in the winter is just bad. I told my girlfriend that February is the worst month of my life.

She replied confused with "It's the shortest month in the year!?"

"Yeah, but it's a suckfest."

Then March comes and gives you about five or six days of hope when we heat wave at 35 - 45 degrees melting snow. But boom, there is always just one more snow storm from mother nature usually at the end of March or early April, just making sure you aren't getting too excited for better weather. You know, when the snow is almost 90% gone, you can see your future getting brighter, then you wake up and Mother Fuckin Nature put white stuff all over your yard. That my friends, is how you get screwed by Wisconsin. Even though I live in Michigan, I blame Wisconsin for a lot of my problems. #damncheeseheads

I just feel like winter is so monotonous. Wake up, coffee, attempt to match, get the kids off to school, head to work, workout, desklife, meetings, home, repeat. But at least in summer, it's like ok summer yes!! Let's get fresh air all night and play in the backyard, go to the beach, take a bike ride, bonfires, smores….. I mean, summer.

#PERSONALDEFEAT

Do you ever struggle real bad. Struggle to get things accomplished, struggle to find an answer or your voice, struggle to make people listen who have no intention of truly understanding what you are trying to say.

Struggle to see your worth when things don't go your way or to find your purpose. I totally believe it's ok to not know what is coming next, but sometimes I feel like I'm stuck and have no idea what way to go. I'm just living. Just merely surviving the rat race of life. Just sweating in the sun, just waking up and going to work, just lifting and trying to eat good. Just being a mom. JUST. I am JUST. But sometimes I want more. I want that drive again. I want that motivation I used to have, that confidence. That my shit doesn't stink back. But in a nice way. Trying to wrap my brain around, when will that fire, that passion and that confidence return. When my worth is at a low I just freeze. I've struggled many times to write this book. I have stopped the process all together for months at a time. I told myself the other day that I'll just let it go, don't write it. How do I even write it? Who will my publisher be? Should I just do it on notebook paper and buy a copy machine? And with those worries, I stopped writing. And if you are reading this right now, you will find out that I did start again…. But what really is the point? It was NEVER my goal or on my bucket list to write a book.

I actually failed, like F, my Freshman English class in college, because I plagiarized. I didn't care, let's copy and paste, then do a beer bong. What am I doing or even proving by writing a book? I was nervous about my cover with my body dysmorphia and haven't even made a professional photo shoot yet, because of these insecurities. Let's just keep it low key. Maybe I shouldn't even write it. Why do people care what I have to say? So many thoughts raced, I am just being super transparent here, but do I even need instagram followers? Do I need to 'market.' I feel weird pretending to be some hot shot that I am not. Maybe just being myself is truly what I need to get back to. And not worry about followers, or getting my book out there. I guess maybe that is why I'm struggling, my fucking book, that I boasted about saying I will write, and here I am, sitting with my thumb up my ass. So many unknowns scare the shit outta me and are holding me back. I'm scared to fail, but there is always that 'what-if' that lingers.

So all you can do when you are stuck and struggling is keep moving. Sometimes taking a break on the couch with a pan of brownies is necessary, but then you need a plan.

Seriously, writers are geniuses. They are genius, beautiful people, who have a story to tell, crazy ass stories sometimes, but they are deep, they are dark, and they wanted to share it. I couldn't imagine being the mom writing *50 Shades of Grey*. Talk about crazy to write something for the first time and it's all sexual, putting out your crooked thoughts into the world not knowing if it will be received the right way? That's what I will do. I will share my story. Whether it be funny, serious, sad, I will share because I can and I do have things to say, that release something within me to feel open and myself. So, I encourage you to do something that scares the shit out of you. Because I think I just pooped my pants.

#CONFIDENCE

I don't think like this everyday, but sometimes I go dark. I go black. Like an out of body experience, but not one where you are looking creepily at yourself. Like glimmers of bad-assness. Where you grow balls, you find your worth, and no-one can take it away from you. I love these moments. And you most definitely can have these moments, months apart, and just love that each time, you embrace more and more worth. You have a serious talk with yourself, think about your happiness, the path that you are on, and what you want to accomplish in your life, or even weekend, I guess. You create your path and it's clear. Serious decisions can be made at this moment, or plans can be laid out. You find your gift. You are reminded of what gets you out of bed in the morning, besides your kids screaming from their bedrooms.

You get one shot, that's it. I think about that from time to time. These people who are so miserable in their relationships and lives. They just settle and that is sad to me. Knowing what I know now, I'd offer advice, but I don't really want people slashing my tires. Like do what you want. Take risks, quit your job, open up a business, take the trip, ask her out, live in your means, take control of your life. Sometimes you take the bumpy road, but you find out, it will get flat, keep moving forward. I suggest jumping. Fucking jump. Don't stay in unfit circumstances for yourself or your family based on fear. Fear of the unknown, fear of being alone, fear of failing. If you're in an unfit circumstance, you are already failing, let's go a little more rock bottom and get low and get back up. Think about your kids. They are your story. They are your legacy you leave behind, how you choose to display how beautiful or scary life is, passes down to them. The way you walk, the way you talk. When you mess up, apologize and actually mean it, then push through. Be better. Always strive to be better.

About 6 months into writing this book, I wasn't very nice to myself. I wasn't being true to myself at all. Trying to do something you have never done before is scary af. Especially if it's something that when you think of it, you say 'yeah, yes I should do that, that sounds like something I would do'. And trying to figure things out with little to no help is scary af. But if it bothers you, that you can't figure it out, and it hurts you to know that you have failed because you have given up, or want to give up. Then it's yours to have. You have to do it

I thought that in order to write this book, I had to be on point. I have to get glamour shots and be witty and have a library full of photos to use for later posts to enlighten my audience. But guess what, that was a big fat fail. That's not real life, that's not what I'm all about. I am a here and now kind of gal, when things come to my head, I write them down. When things inspire me, I take a picture and write about the feeling I have at that moment. Maybe I am writing everything that every person out there is thinking. And cough cough, I'm not the only crazy one out there! Sure girl power, blah blah blah. But to have girl power, in a small community, where you can all relate to something, that's cool. Unicorn magic. Now I'm not saying I'm David Copperfield, but have you ever seen both of us in the same room?

The reason why this book is even happening is because of you guys. When I get out of my head, and let my mind wander, that's when I can clearly see and think. Forget all those perfect instagram bitches doing the 15 in 15, or whatever bullshit they do. Forget the physique models that have a perfect ass. I will never be that, we will NEVER be that. Don't correct me if I'm wrong, but I think like only 10% of Americans actually look like Barbie. Well, ok, not Barbie, but they say something crazy like all those fitness people you see on Insta selling you shit, are the few and far between.

So, why am I trying to be like everyone else? Why do I want to imitate? I'm not perfect, nobody is. So the fact that I thought I had to be, makes me shake my head. Why did I think that? I sure as fuck hope you guys see my flaws, and see that even though maybe, just maybe, I take five or seven photos of myself to get the right one for my feelings to share. I have cellulite like crazy on my thighs, I have arm jiggles, I yell at my kids, I miss road turns because I'm day dreaming and I get denied by guys, alot.

The thing about confidence is that it doesn't stay forever. It messes with your head. It makes you think you can do things in that moment, which you then do, and after your eyes get really big and you are like wtf just happened. And you have to live and deal with the sexy messy oozness that is your ego. That was me earlier today. I've been kind of depressed, just not myself lately, so trying to get the motivation to even get dressed today, which I didn't, I wore my pajama's all day, was very hard. Something eventually got all up in me though... it must have been the double dose of doughnuts and cappuccino that rushed through my head when I made the declaration. So declaring to the world that I was going to publish a book this coming year, I had about 20 seconds of extreme courage, and saw past the black hole I was swimming in and well, that was it. Declared. Now, I didn't say how many pages it would actually be. But, it would be, in fact a book.

I like quotes. They give me hope, they give me strength and make me do some stupidly wonderful things. "Sometimes all you need is 20 seconds of insane courage. Just literally 20 seconds of just embarrassing bravery, and I promise you, something great will come of it." One of the quotes I revert to when I need to really dig deep and do something scary and exhilarating. It's from *We Bought a Zoo*. But maybe it stemmed from somewhere else first.

There is no background on me and writing. I've always been an art nerd. I went to Central Michigan University (Fire Up Chips) knowing I wanted to dabble in art, but by the end of my Freshman year, I knew I wanted to get into graphic design. The computer helped me design, where my hands couldn't. Although I'm an art major, I personally felt I couldn't draw or paint for crap. So I guess I've always had that artsy dark edge, the ability to take movies and songs and feel and hear the pain in the singers voice. Artists are all the same in all different types of media. Whether it's painting, writing, drawing, singing, or designing. etc. We all have this inner pain, this inner fire inside of us that needs to communicate less through words and show through with art. Writing is my other escape. I remember in art class, that was my outlet in College. Whatever I was feeling, or going through at that time in my life, I would paint it, or glue things together, or sing in my car, Avril Lavigne on repeat. Girl got me.

If you ever meet me in person, you won't see the writer. You'll see someone else. At least that's what I think. I'm not this crazy deep dark soul analyzing every second of my day. Wait, yeah I can be. A lot of the time, I don't know what day it is, my legs are never shaved, I have sweaty clothes on, and I'm going from point A to point B constantly. But when I sit down, with total silence or the birds, let my mind wander, my brain reacts, and weird deep thoughts come to me. So there's that.

Whatever you get out of this book, I hope you are able to use it in some form. Even if it's one chapter. But please, if you enjoy this book, pass it along. I do apologize for using the F bomb, sometimes you just have to. Maybe when you are done, you can bury this in the sand or in a public place where someone can clearly find it, making their day with a simple note just as - enjoy this book, sign your name on the inside of the cover and pass it along, just as I have"

#OUTRO

What I came across when I googled 'How to write a book' was this: *Nobody cares about the book you almost wrote. As you approach the end of this project, know that this will be hard and you will most certainly mess up. Just be okay with failing and give yourself grace. That's what will sustain you - the determination will continue, not your elusive standards of perfect.* These are the words I lived off during this process.

"Alexa: how do you write a book?"

ABOUT THE AUTHOR

Allyson Bickel was born and raised in the Upper Peninsula of Michigan. For those that do not know, it is Michigan's *better half.* Living one hour from Green Bay, WI, and two and a half hours from Milwaukee, she cheers on the Packers and Brew Crew. She looks cool in whatever she wears, she's not wearing anything yellow. (Remember Dream Phone?)

Allyson is a mix of fire and ice. She is an extrovert who loves human connection and shenanigans. Allyson was never an aspiring writer and even failed her English 101 Course at Central Michigan University. Fire Up Chips! She raises two children the best she can and tries to see the best in each situation until she can't and then just needs to swear.

Made in the USA
Coppell, TX
02 August 2020

32250779R20065